SEPTEMBER TIDE

SEPTEMBER

a play in three acts

TIDE

by Daphne du Maurier

DOUBLEDAY & COMPANY, INC., GARDEN CITY, N.Y., 1950

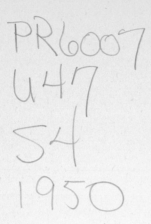

PR6007
U47
S4
1950

TO MY MOTHER

September Tide was first produced at the New Theatre, Oxford, on November 8th, 1948. Its first performance in the West End of London was at the Aldwych Theatre on December 15th, 1948. The cast was as follows:

STELLA MARTYN, *Gertrude Lawrence*
CHERRY, *Anne Leon*
EVAN DAVIES, *Michael Gough*
JIMMY, *Bryan Forbes*
ROBERT HANSON, *Cyril Raymond*
MRS. TUCKET, *Dandy Nicols*

Produced by Irene Hentschel

CHARACTERS

STELLA MARTYN

CHERRY, *Stella's daughter*

EVAN DAVIES, *Stella's son-in-law*

JIMMY, *Stella's son*

ROBERT HANSON, *A friend of the family*

MRS. TUCKET, *A daily woman*

SCENES

SEPTEMBER TIDE

ACT 1

The action of the play takes place in the living-room of the house, and in the studio. The living-room is a long, low room, with cream washed walls and a stone-flagged floor. Part of the natural rock, against which the house is built can be seen L. There is a fire-place L. and beyond this a door leading to the hall. Back L. a cupboard for drinks, and a desk. Back centre R. and L. are small windows looking out upon the harbour, and in middle centre a door to the slipway with a hatch window, which is nearly always open. R. by R. window is a small grand piano, and behind this a flight of steps leading to the studio or attic. There is a sofa and a chair near the fire. There should be a distinct atmosphere of the sea about the room: we must know this, and should be aware of the fact that the house is right on the harbour's edge, and looks out on to the estuary itself. We might hear the sound of ships occasionally, or the lap of water at high tide. There might even be the crying of gulls.

There are flowers on the table, and flowers, too, on the piano, but nothing feminine or fussy about the room.

Prawning nets in a corner, and possibly seaboots, and oilskins hanging somewhere. There might be a work-basket on a corner of the sofa, and some mending, because the house belongs to a woman. It is her home, and a happy one.

The living-room, about six o'clock of a summer evening. The stage is empty. The sun comes through the open hatch door leading to the slipway. Sound of gulls perhaps, and in the far distance the hooting of a tug at the mouth of the harbour.

MRS. TUCKET *enters at door L. from hall. She is a plump, cheerful-looking woman, with a large bosom and probably untidy hair. Wears an apron over her frock. She is carrying a basket of logs, and is singing a verse from "Jerusalem." Places log basket by fire, then goes to cupboard and fetches glasses and a tray. Straightens seaboots and prawning nets, then— Exits again L.*

As she does so, someone from the slipway whistles and calls "Stella." A man looks through the open hatchway. It is ROBERT HANSON, *the friend of the family. He is fifty-ish, but probably looks older. Either grey-haired or going bald. The kind of man who would be invaluable in times of trouble or sudden illness. Kind, dependable, safe and stolid. Not very much sense of humour, and never exciting, but so nice.*

ROBERT: Hullo there, Stella? Anybody home?

He comes in through hatch door, sees tray with glasses on it. He smiles, and produces a bottle of whisky from under his arm, wrapped up in a piece of newspaper. Places this on table. MRS. TUCKET *enters L.*

Good evening, Mrs. Tucket.

MRS. T.: Oh, good evening, Mr. Hanson. Mrs. Martyn has just gone up the village to see if she can get any whisky from the Ferry Inn.

ROBERT: I could have saved her the journey, Mrs. Tucket. Just remembered I had this hidden away in a locker on my boat.

MRS. T. (*admiring*): Proper job, sir. Mrs. Martyn *will* be pleased. She had half a bottle of gin, but it seemed that Mr. Davies won't touch anything but whisky.

ROBERT: H'm. You have to take what you can get these days, and be damn thankful for it.

MRS. T.: That's right, sir. But you know what Mrs. Martyn is. If Master Jimmy or Miss Cherry ask for any mortal thing they have to have it, and now it will be the same with Mr. Davies. We've been turning the place upside down all day to get straight. Shifting the other bed into Miss Cherry's room, and I don't know what else. Not that I mind hard work, I've been used to it all my life, not like these local women. "That's why I married you, Dolly," my poor Tom used to say. "When you get down to a job, you get down to it, and no messing about."

ROBERT: H'm. I'm sure Mrs. Martyn will be very grateful for your help, and Miss Cherry, too. But I was forgetting, we mustn't call her Miss Cherry any more, must we? She's Mrs. Davies now.

MRS. T.: Mrs. Davies. It will take a bit of getting used to.

ROBERT: Mrs. Martyn is very excited, I suppose?

MRS. T.: Over the moon, sir. Talking about grandchildren already, and how she's going to build a new wing on to the house between the kitchen and the garage. You've no idea! You've seen what she's done to the attic?

MRS. TUCKET *nods to the steps up R.*

ROBERT: No? What's she done?

MRS. T.: Turned it into a studio for Mr. Davies. Did the whole thing in two days. You wouldn't recognise it. Distempered the walls herself. You know what it was, nothing but an old lumber loft, where Master Jimmy used to play on wet days. Will you take a peep at it?

ROBERT: I think I'd better wait until Mr. Davies invites me.

MRS. T. (*taking newspaper from table*): There's quite a bit about him in the *Western Morning News*. With his photograph, too. Have you seen it? (*Shows him the paper.*)

ROBERT: Yes, I saw it at the Club.

MRS. T.: Quite famous he seems to be, doesn't he? Pictures in the Leicester Gallery, just near the Odeon Cinema. Have you ever seen any of them?

ROBERT: No; I can't say I have.

MRS. T. (*laughing, folding newspaper*): Boats are more in your line, aren't they, sir? Well, it's lovely for Miss Cherry to be married, and lovely for her mother to have her home again. Do you know what Mrs. Martyn said to me, though?

ROBERT: What did she say?

MRS. T.: "Oh, Mrs. Tucket," she said—this was after Miss Cherry had rung her up, you know, to say they'd been to the Registry Office—"I'm so happy about Miss Cherry, but I do wish she'd have come home sooner, and had a proper old-fashioned wedding down here."

ROBERT: Not much chance of an old-fashioned wedding with a girl like Miss Cherry for a daughter, and an artist for a son-in-law, Mrs. Tucket.

We feel he vaguely disapproves of the marriage.

18

MRS. T.: No, sir, I suppose not. And then Miss Cherry was always one for having her own way. Living up in London on her own and going in for painting, the way she's been doing this past year. Anything might have happened to her. Being in the W.R.N.S. unsettled her, I shall always say that. But Mrs. Martyn won't hear a word against her.

ROBERT: Spoilt. That's always been the trouble. The same with the brother, too. But perhaps the Navy will lick some of the nonsense out of him. Their mother's been too good to the pair of them, always, since the father died. Never a thought for herself all these years.

MRS. T.: You're right there, sir. No. I always say there's no one like Mrs. Martyn.

Pause.

ROBERT: Well . . . I suppose they'll be here any moment now.

He moves to hatch and stands there shading his eyes, looking out.

I can see the Ferry coming across now, and someone who looks very much like Miss Cherry standing up in the boat.

MRS. TUCKET *moves to hatch beside him.*

MRS. T.: Oh! That's them, sir. The train must have been very punctual for once. We heard from the station this morning it had been running as much as an hour late. Oh, Mrs. Martyn *will* be vexed that she's not here to greet them. (*Fusses around.*)

ROBERT: I should go up to the village if I were you——

MRS. T.: I think I'd better.

19

ROBERT: —and warn her that the happy pair are about to descend upon her.

MRS. T.: Won't you stay, sir?

ROBERT: Not on your life! (*Goes out of hatch door.*) I'll look in later, when they're settling down, and the ice has been broken. Besides, I've got to put my boat to bed. Good evening, Mrs. Tucket.

MRS. T.: Good evening, sir.

ROBERT exits through hatch. MRS. TUCKET, with a quick look round, exits L. The scene is empty again, as at the beginning. The gulls cry. Presently we hear the excited voice of a girl laughing.

EVAN (*off L.*): What's this bogus bit of nautical nonsense?

CHERRY (*off L.*): It's not bogus; it's genuine. It's a real ship's bell that we pinched off an old schooner when she was falling to bits up the river, and we've used it for a door bell ever since. Mother! Where are you?

Through the door L. comes CHERRY. She is about twenty-three, pretty, with short curly hair like a boy and a general boyish appearance about her. She wears a pale blue suit; no hat.

Mother? Mother? (*Looks round room and calls over her shoulder.*) Evan! Mother isn't here. I think she's forgotten all about us. Oh, letters!

She turns, laughing to EVAN, who comes in L. He is about thirty-eight, but often looks rather younger. An arresting face, sensitive, aware. He stands at the entrance, looking about the room. CHERRY darts at the table. Sees letters there.

Mrs. Davies. . . . Mrs. Davies. . . . Mrs. Davies. . . . Why does a simple thing like marriage make one's friends gloat so frightfully? I can't possibly answer them

all. And, anyway, I shouldn't know what to say. . . .
Oh, whisky. Evan, how wonderful! And how exactly
like Mother to remember. (*She turns and looks at him.*)
What's the matter?

EVAN: This room. . . . You described it very badly.

CHERRY: Did I? Are you disappointed?

EVAN: God, no. . . . (*He looks all round.*) It's quite perfect. The sort of room I've always wanted.

CHERRY (*delighted*): But I *told* you it was lovely. You
never listen to a word I say. I'm certain you imagined it
was going to be a fearful seaside villa, with a flag-pole
in the garden and ferns in the hall. (*She goes to hatch
and leans out.*) You've no idea what bliss it is to be
home again. (*She waves wildly.*) Hoo-ey . . . Robert
. . . Hoo-ey. (*Laughs over shoulder to* EVAN.) There
goes Robert, Mother's faithful boy-friend, pulling out
to his boat against the devil of a tide. I can never
decide which he loves most, his boat or Mother.
(*Shouts*) Robert! How are you? Come and have a
drink?

EVAN: Oh, for Lord's sake. . . . Don't start throwing par-
ties. It's all I can do to face my mother-in-law.

CHERRY: Robert's not a party, and you'll have to meet him
some time. He runs everything down here, from the
Cottage Hospital to the Boy Scouts. He's rather pomp-
ous and a perfect pet. And I've told you a thousand
times that Mother's the easiest thing in the world. . . .
Just like a cosy cup of tea.

EVAN: But I don't like cups of tea. I detest them. (*Walks
to table and picks up whisky.*)

CHERRY: Well, she's remembered your whisky, anyway.
Surely that's one good mark in her favour. Mother
never forgets anything. I'll have some of the gin. (*They*

pour drinks.) As to her cooking, it's positively *cordon bleu*. Entirely self-taught during the war. No austerity nonsense. And, yes—what did I tell you? There's a wood fire burning, even though it is midsummer. You can't imagine, Evan, what it is for Jimmy and me to come down here and relax, and know that we don't have to do a damn thing because Mother will do it for us all. Even down to the mending of our underpants.

EVAN: Knowing the state of yours, I should think they keep her very busy.

CHERRY: Oh, I can't be bothered with things like that. Never could thread a needle and never will. But Mother's old-fashioned. Lavender and lace practically. Thoroughly domestic. I always tell her she ought to have lived a hundred years ago, and worn mittens.

EVAN: You fill me more and more with apprehension, I shan't know what to say to her at all.

CHERRY: You needn't utter, if you don't feel like it. Mother will rattle on quite happily. And, like all that generation, she has a mind like a sink. Enjoys nothing so much as a good lavatory joke.

EVAN: My stock of closet jests is very small. And whatever sense of humour I started out with on this venture is fast vanishing, and if it wasn't for the quite unexpected charm of this room, and the view of the harbour, I'd cross that ferry again and catch the next train back to London.

CHERRY: You couldn't do anything so incredibly vile and mean. (*Pause. She looks up towards steps R.*) I wonder —what did she mean about a surprise in the attic?

Puts down glass. Goes up steps and into studio. EVAN *leans over hatch-door, drinking his whisky and looking over harbour.* CHERRY *gives a cry of delight from above.*

Oh! Evan. . . .

EVAN (*not turning round*): What's the matter?

CHERRY: You can't imagine. She's turned the attic into a studio. Come and see. (*She comes to top of steps and looks down at* EVAN.)

EVAN: I don't want a studio. I want to look at this view.

CHERRY: You have the same view from here, only better. You simply must come. Quickly.

EVAN (*smiling and putting down glass*): All right, all right. What's the old lady done? Bought me a box of paints and a lay figure? I didn't come down here to paint. I came to lie in the sun and catch mackerel.

CHERRY: You can't lie in the sun down in Cornwall. It rains every other day. And the mackerel have all disappeared to the East Coast. Besides, you've got to work. I only married you because you're famous, and you can't possibly let me down.

EVAN *laughs, and bending over piano, strikes a chord as though to test it.*

(*Impatiently*) Oh, come on.

EVAN *goes to steps and walks up them to studio.*

EVAN (*good-natured*): Now then, what's it all about?

He stands in doorway of studio and gives a whistle of surprise.

I say! This is fun.

CHERRY: What did I tell you? (*She was very pleased.*) Oh, what the hell is Mother doing? It's so unlike her not to be on the spot with open arms. I wonder if she can have gone up the village for anything? (*She comes down steps into living-room.*)

EVAN (*following her down*): Let her stay there, then. The thought of being face to face with a mother-in-law at last is making me remember every music-hall joke I've ever heard. What did I do with my junk?

CHERRY: Dumped it all in the hall. Don't you want to see the rest of the house? (*She goes L. to hall.*)

EVAN: Not particularly. I don't propose ever moving from this room. Come and help me carry up my stuff.

CHERRY (*appearing with suitcases and coats*): Here it is.

EVAN: Look out with that coat. There's a bottle of whisky in the pocket. (*Picks up bags and coats, taking whisky bottle from pocket and putting it on table beside the other.*)

CHERRY: You are *awful!* (*Looks at whisky bottles.*) Don't get plastered too early, will you? I want you to make a good impression.

EVAN: I shall get plastered just as soon as it suits me. In fact, with this ordeal in front of me, the earlier I begin, the better for all concerned. (*Has another drink from his glass, and then moves up the steps to studio, with bags and coats.*)

CHERRY: Well, in that case, I'll leave you to it and warn Mother what to expect. She can't be far away. (*She exits L.*)

EVAN: If she's doling out chicken broth to some old cripple, let her stay. I can look after myself.

EVAN *goes into hall, and comes back carrying some packages and an easel. Leaves easel at bottom of steps and carries packages up to studio. Vague sounds of cases and things being moved about in the studio. In a moment or two* STELLA *appears at the door of hatchway.*

24

*She is quite different from the sort of mother we have
expected. Although her hair is going silver-grey, her
face is youthful and very lovely, and she has large eyes
which express almost all the things that pass through
her mind. Thus, when she looks at anyone, we must
know what she is thinking. And when she smiles, her
heart is laid bare. She is dressed in a linen frock, probably years old, but very good still, and very becoming:
short sleeves, probably a scarf, no hat. She looks round
the room, smiles as she sees the disorder of arrival. She
carries a bunch of roses and a bottle of whisky. She sees
the other two bottles of whisky on the table and mur-
murs, "Oh, thank goodness!" Goes to bottom of steps
and examines luggage. In doing so, she brushes against
easel and sends it crashing to the ground.*

(Shouting from inside studio) For God's sake, don't
touch my things.

STELLA *looks up, rather alarmed. Replaces easel.* EVAN
comes out on to steps.

EVAN *(as he comes)*: What *are* you doing? *(He then sees it
is* STELLA *who stands below and not* CHERRY, *as he
thought. He stands staring at her. We must feel that she
is as great a surprise to him as she was to us. He doesn't
say anything.)*

STELLA, *a little shy, is the first to recover.*

STELLA: How do you do? . . . I'm Mother.

EVAN *comes slowly down the steps towards her.*

EVAN: How do you do.

STELLA: Do I kiss you?

EVAN: I don't know.

She kisses him. Then steps back and looks at him.

STELLA: It's rather absurd. I've no idea how one behaves. I've never had a son-in-law before.

EVAN: Perhaps I'm only the first of a long series.

They both smile. This somehow breaks the ice.

STELLA: I've brought you some roses for your studio. The one thing I had forgotten. And I wasn't quite sure if you would like them or not. Not knowing about artists.

EVAN: But I do like them. Very much.

She puts roses on table, where there are now three bottles of whisky.

STELLA: Where's Cherry?

EVAN: Gone to look for you.

STELLA: I went up to the village to get some whisky. Cherry said you drank an awful lot. Do you?

EVAN: I'm afraid I do.

STELLA: I wish it wasn't so difficult to get. I shall have to go round bribing people. I only drink myself when I have to face anything rather terrible, like speaking at the Woman's Institute or talking to the Bishop. I rather feel like drinking something now.

EVAN (*laughing outright*): Am I as bad as that?

STELLA (*distressed*): Oh, dear! How very rude of me.

EVAN (*pouring her out a drink*): It isn't rude at all. It's the most natural thing in the world to be apprehensive about the stranger who has pitched head first out of the blue into your home.

26

STELLA: I wasn't apprehensive. Just . . . curious.

She takes her drink, and looks at him. He fills up his glass.

You see, all this has been very exciting for me. I live alone so much. I have the misfortune to be one of those mothers who are idiotic about their children.

EVAN: So I gather.

STELLA (*swallowing her drink*): And it all happened so suddenly. I never thought Cherry would marry. Or at any rate, not for years. So if I suddenly become hysterical, and burst into tears, you mustn't take any notice of me.

EVAN: Except to give you more whisky.

She smiles, and shakes her head.

STELLA: Oh! but I'm happy. Really happy.

EVAN: Are you? So am I.

They move to sofa. STELLA *sits down.*

STELLA: Of course, Cherry mentioned you casually from time to time in letters; but I'd no idea there was anything serious between you. You know you're quite different from that photograph in the papers—that awful beard.

EVAN: Very old photograph. I haven't worn a beard for years.

STELLA: And must promise never to again.

EVAN: I don't make promises. One of my rules.

STELLA: Oh! I see. A difficult man.

27

EVAN (*firmly*): Very.

STELLA: Faddy about your food?

EVAN: Extremely.

STELLA (*apprehensive*): Allergic to lobster?

EVAN: Can't touch it.

STELLA: Then you won't get any supper tonight.

EVAN (*laughing*): Don't worry. Lobster, in any form, is my favourite dish.

STELLA: Truly? Not, with sauce *à l'American?*

EVAN: Lovely.

STELLA: And artichokes to follow?

EVAN: The globe kind? (*Gestures with his hands.*) The edges rather curled, not too green, melted butter?

STELLA (*delighted*): Yes.

EVAN: One of my passions. How could you know?

STELLA: Intuition. My one quality. I've no brains at all, as Cherry has probably told you.

EVAN: Cherry has told me nothing. Or what she has done, was completely wrong.

He sits down on sofa beside her.

STELLA: Why did you marry my precious daughter?

EVAN: She cleans my paint-brushes better than I do myself.

STELLA (*rather shaken*): How interesting. Is that all you demand in a wife?

EVAN: Not quite all. Cherry is invaluable at answering the telephone, and telling people I've left London when I haven't. And, incidentally, she knows a good picture from a bad one.

STELLA: Ah! That—surely—is very important.

EVAN: Very. Especially when we go round looking at other people's pictures. Like all artists, I dislike being told the truth about my own.

STELLA: Of course, she thinks everything you do is wonderful.

EVAN: By no means. She is far too intelligent for that. But she grades my work as being about fifteen per cent. better than anybody else's, which I find flattering and even comforting. You see, the war took quite a slice out of my painting life. Droning backwards and forwards in a bomber is hardly conducive to creative talent. I've got to make up for all that now.

STELLA: You seem to be succeeding—judging by the newspapers. And what about Cherry? Has she any talent, do you think?

EVAN: You want me to be frank?

STELLA: Please. I should hate a son-in-law to be anything else.

EVAN: Cherry can turn out quite a pretty little greeting card. A spray of lilies in an ebony vase. That's about the form.

STELLA (*chastened*): I see. . . . What a blessing that she didn't go in for singing. Such an expensive training. The

Art School was comparatively cheap—apart from the flat in Chelsea. However, if she has learnt to clean your brushes, then the family savings haven't been entirely thrown away.

EVAN: On the contrary. They've been invested. And I forgot to tell you another admirable thing about Cherry that I discovered quite early in our acquaintance. She knows all the pubs in Chelsea where one can buy whisky by the bottle.

STELLA: The W.R.N.S. were supposed to encourage initiative. She certainly didn't learn that at St. Mary's. . . . (*She rises.*) Well, it's all very exciting and thrilling for you both, but I can't help feeling that young people nowadays, like you and Cherry, get married for rather strange reasons. Quite different from the reasons I got married for in nineteen twenty-five.

EVAN (*gravely*): Quite different. You see, the things you got married for in nineteen twenty-five were still comparatively difficult to obtain without marriage. In nineteen forty-eight they're handed to you without asking.

STELLA (*rather prim*): I don't think I know what you mean.

EVAN: I'm delighted to hear it. (*Swallows drink.*)

STELLA (*looking at bottles*): It's a good thing we have three of those. Cherry and I will stick to lemonade.

EVAN: What happens when we run dry?

STELLA: We go across to the Ferry Inn, and you will pay. Tell me—do you like your studio? (*She arranges flowers on piano.*)

EVAN: I like everything. The harbour. The view. My studio. And this room above all. (*Motions with his hands.*) All your doing?

STELLA: Yes.

EVAN: Intuition again?

STELLA: I suppose so. Houses and food and looking after people has always been my job. Like painting is yours. I'm very ignorant, you know. I know nothing about it.

EVAN: Know nothing about what?

STELLA: About painting.

EVAN: You don't have to.

He looks at her all the while she talks. Not with insolence or familiarity, but because he finds her lovely.

STELLA (*reminiscent*): I remember falling in love with an artist once. I was eighteen at the time. But he was an unsuccessful artist. Not a famous one like you.

EVAN: What happened to him?

STELLA: I don't know. I married a sailor instead. (*She laughs at him with her eyes.*)

EVAN: Very wise of you. What decided you?

STELLA (*sitting down on chair near piano*): All that gold braid; and knowing there would be crossed swords at the wedding.

EVAN: A shallow girl. No deep emotions.

STELLA: Not in those days. A uniform meant everything. Even the policeman's at the corner! Tell me. (*Serious.*) You are going to make Cherry happy, aren't you?

EVAN: I haven't thought about it.

STELLA: Then it's time you did.

EVAN *puts his glass down on table.*

EVAN: How do I start?

STELLA: By letting her know she is the most important thing in your life, of course.

EVAN: But she isn't.

STELLA: Oh!

EVAN: My work is much more important.

STELLA: In that case, I'll have another drink.

EVAN *laughs and fills her glass. But* STELLA *is solemn.*

No, I'm serious. This isn't a joking matter. Especially where my only daughter is concerned. Marriage is a very solemn thing.

EVAN: It's not worth being solemn about anything in the year of grace nineteen forty-eight.

STELLA: Nonsense. What has this year of grace got to do with marriage? Atom bombs and Russia, I suppose you mean? That's just an excuse for careless behaviour. And post-war standards are always slovenly. Thank Heaven I had Puritan parents who brought me up to have a pre-1914 mentality. My marriage was a very happy one for that reason.

EVAN: I wonder.

STELLA: What do you wonder?

EVAN: If that was the reason you were happy. I doubt if nineteen-fourteen standards had anything to do with it.

STELLA: Give me a better reason then.

EVAN looks at her as though he were about to say something, then changes his mind, and says it in a different way.

EVAN: Blessed are the pure in heart, for they shall see God.

STELLA: I think that's blasphemous.

EVAN: Very probably.

Sound of CHERRY calling "Mother" from the hall. She comes into the room, followed by the dog.

STELLA: Darling. (*She rises from the sofa and goes to CHERRY.*)

They hug each other. EVAN watches them.

Oh! I think I'm going to cry.

CHERRY (*laughing and hugging STELLA*): Don't be such an idiot. What the hell is there to cry about?

STELLA: Everything! (*Laughs, blows her nose, kisses CHERRY again, and looks apologetically at EVAN.*) You see? I warned you this would happen.

EVAN smiles. STELLA moves to fireplace. CHERRY follows her.

CHERRY: You're so incredibly sentimental, dearest. Weddings, christenings, the white ensign on a battleship, God save the King—everything reduces you to a state of pulp. Look at you. You're in a complete flap. I know all the signs. Hair out of place, hands shaking . . .

EVAN: That's the whisky.

CHERRY: You haven't been giving her whisky. Absolutely fatal!

STELLA (*laughing, patting her hair*): How horrible you are!
(*Sits on sofa with* CHERRY.)

CHERRY: There I've been sweating up the village to look for
you, and all the while you've been sitting here getting
sozzled with my husband. You ought to be ashamed of
yourself. (*Cuddling up to her.*) Well? What do you
think of him? Nicer than you expected?

STELLA: Much.

EVAN: What did you expect?

STELLA: That bearded man in the newspaper, with long
hair falling down his collar.

EVAN: Sandals and dirty toe-nails. I know. As a matter of
fact, I invariably wear sandals in the house, but not the
toe-less kind. I shall go and put them on at once. Also a
very good line in scarves, instead of this collar and tie,
which is choking me.

STELLA: Oh, wonderful! I do want him to look artistic for
Robert. He'll be in directly.

EVAN (*picking up easel at foot of steps*): Who is Robert?

CHERRY (*getting drink and cigarette*): You know, I told
you. Mother's old boy-friend. He's adored her ever since
Daddy died, and probably before that. He proposes
regularly once a month. It's "routes."

EVAN: What is "routes"?

CHERRY: One of Mother's private words for something that
happens with unfailing regularity, like the new moon, or
the turn of the tide.

STELLA: My code word for "routine."

EVAN: I see. Then if it is "routes" for the luckless Robert to propose, it is also "routes" for you to refuse?

STELLA: But of course!

EVAN: Another Cornish rhapsody!

He goes up to studio.

STELLA (*calling*): If you want to change now, Cherry will show you your room.

EVAN (*calling back*): But this *is* my room.

STELLA (*to* CHERRY): Darling, I've put you both together, of course. I've moved Jimmy's bed into your room, and shifted the wardrobe between the windows, and . . .

CHERRY (*interrupting*): Damn. I ought to have told you. We don't sleep together, you know.

STELLA (*disconcerted*): Oh!

CHERRY: What I mean is, we don't share a room. Evan loathes it. . . . He's so fastidious. He says it's the end of everything.

STELLA: It wasn't in my day.

CHERRY: Your day was different.

STELLA: It must have been!

CHERRY: Besides, you must remember Evan is an artist. And artists are not like other men.

STELLA (*interested*): Aren't they? *Do* tell me.

CHERRY: Don't say "Do tell me" in that beady way, as though there was something queer about Evan. Really,

Mother, your generation is absolutely riddled with sex. You think of nothing else.

STELLA (*hurt*): We're not. And I don't.

CHERRY: All you have to do is to put sheets and things on that perfectly good divan in the studio. He's quite crazy about that room already.

STELLA (*doubtfully*): But it will mean he will have to come trailing down here in the dark, and across the hall, and up the staircase, if he wants to go to your room.

CHERRY: What of it?

STELLA (*firmly*): Daddy would never have done that for me.

CHERRY: Oh, well, what's the odds. If Evan wants to go paddling around in the dark, it's his funeral.

STELLA (*giggling*): I think it very probably will be! (*Moves away.*)

CHERRY (*sternly*): You have had too much whisky. Darling, you are naughty. You know how one drink flies to your head.

STELLA (*indignant*): It doesn't. I've got a very strong head. Much stronger than yours, if you want to be personal. And *I* was perfectly sober when I became engaged to be married, and I'm beginning to suspect that you were not (*joking*).

CHERRY (*lies back on sofa*): I know, sweetheart. You were on a yacht at Cowes, there was a full moon, someone played the Eton boating-song ashore, and Daddy said to you, "Why can't this go on for ever?" Quite different from Evan and me. It was pouring with rain in the King's road, and we were both stinking.

STELLA: How terribly unromantic.

CHERRY (*laughing*): Nonsense. It was the greatest fun. Evan spouted reams from *Hamlet,* and nearly fell in the gutter. It was then that his latch-key sank down a drain, and he had to come back and spend the night with me.

STELLA: I don't believe a word of it. You always exaggerated since the age of three when you pretended Nannie beat you with a flat iron. Absolutely untrue. She was a strict Nonconformist and adored you.

CHERRY: She was a fiend and used to strap Jimmy and me to our beds with electric wires! And, anyway, Evan and I *did* get engaged walking down the King's road, in an alcoholic haze. Actually, we can neither of us remember whether it was that night or the next morning we decided to get married.

STELLA (*walking about*): That night, I should hope. . . . Darling, had I realised this was the sort of thing you were doing in Chelsea, I should never have allowed you to take that flat.

CHERRY: Why on earth not? It was all perfectly harmless. If you love a person who gets tiddley, the least you can do is to take him back home and give him your bed.

STELLA (*rather prim*): Well . . . I can't help feeling very relieved that everything has ended as it has done.

CHERRY (*sitting up, looking mischievous*): It saves a lot of trouble, doesn't it? Getting married, I mean. If you want to travel or go anywhere. Amazing how stuffy some hotels can still be about things like that. Funnily enough, Brighton, which you would think would be dead easy, is awfully sticky, and Cumberland, on the contrary, which is full of Methodists, money for jam.

STELLA (*shocked*): Cherry—you don't mean to say—you actually went away with Evan, ever, before you were actually married?

CHERRY (*surprised*): But, of course. Damn it all darling, I've known Evan for ages. Quite six months. What would you expect us to do at week-ends? Go to Kew?

STELLA (*shrugging her shoulders*): I don't pretend to understand what goes on nowadays. It's utterly beyond me. Why, if I had done such a thing when I was your age—I just don't know what would have happened.

CHERRY (*smiling*): I do. A nervous breakdown, or a baby. Probably both. I told you just now, your generation was riddled with sex. Thank God we're different. And, anyway, those few days that Evan and I spent in Cumberland, we went for long walks all the time and discussed Van Gogh.

STELLA: What about the evenings?

CHERRY: Played gin rummy and slept like logs.

STELLA: Then I can't think why you bothered to go to Cumberland. . . . Oh, all right. Don't make that face at me. If your behaviour was unorthodox before you were married, it's even more unorthodox now. Come and get the sheets from the linen cupboard. Mrs. Tucket will be frightfully shocked in the morning.

CHERRY: Shocked? What on earth about?

STELLA: Married only a fortnight, and separate rooms? Of course she'll be shocked.

CHERRY (*amazed*): Disgusting old woman.

They exit L. into hall. And a few moments afterwards EVAN *comes down into the living-room. He has sandals on, and another jacket, and a vivid scarf round his neck instead of a collar. He goes to table, and examines the whisky bottles gravely. Looks at the opened one, and says, "H'm," ruminating at its already diminished state. Replaces it on table, and, seizing the two unopened ones, he carries them both up the steps to his studio. Returns again, and pours out more whisky from the open bottle into his glass. With his vivid scarf round his neck, and the whisky bottle in his hand, he presents rather a Bohemian appearance to* ROBERT HANSON, *who at this moment puts his head round the hatch door.*

ROBERT: Oh, good evening. You're Cherry's husband, I take it.

EVAN (*turning round*): I am. Come in, won't you? Have a drink?

ROBERT: Seeing that it's my whisky you're making so free with, I think I will.

EVAN: Yours? But how extraordinarily kind of you. Are you the landlord of the Ferry Inn?

ROBERT: I am not. My name is Robert Hanson, and I'm a very old friend of your mother-in-law's.

EVAN (*nodding his head wisely*): Ah! Yes, of course. "Routes."

ROBERT: I beg your pardon?

EVAN (*mysterious*): The new moon. The turn of the tide. Have some of your own whisky? It will give you courage for the next time.

EVAN *hands* ROBERT *a drink.* ROBERT *receives it in silence, disapproving. He feels that* EVAN *has had too much already, and he is probably right.*

(*Waving* ROBERT *to a chair, already host*) Have you come to supper?

ROBERT: No. Merely to offer my congratulations.

EVAN: What about?

ROBERT: On your marriage, of course.

EVAN: Rather early for congratulations, isn't it? I should keep them for at least six months. The whole affair might turn out to be a fearful flop.

ROBERT: H'm. (*Looks more disapproving than ever.*)

EVAN (*sitting on arm of sofa*): I mean, the whole thing of marriage is a toss-up, isn't it? You remember the old story about the man who married the opera singer? After their wedding night, he took one look at her next morning and said, "For God's sake, sing." I always think that tale expresses what most women, and some men, invariably feel on these occasions.

ROBERT: Seems to me a very cynical attitude to take.

EVAN: Do you? (*Swallows drink.*) We must get together sometime and discuss the whole subject.

ROBERT *looks as though this was the last thing in the world he would ever discuss.*

ROBERT: You met Cherry in London, I believe? Some party or other?

EVAN: I don't remember a party. Never go to 'em. Cherry wandered in to one of my favourite bars one evening, and I bought her a drink.

ROBERT (*drily*): When I was young, that was the sort of thing that used to happen in Leicester Square.

EVAN: It probably still does. We're more respectable in Chelsea. The girls follow up with a proposal of marriage.

ROBERT: I'm afraid I'm very old-fashioned. That line of talk is rather beyond me. The war doesn't seem to have improved manners or morals. A pity, I think.

EVAN: Manners are lousy, I grant you. But morals are pretty much where they always were. To the pure, all things are impure. But don't run away with the idea that Cherry led a loose life in Chelsea. As far as I know she was amazingly unattached for a girl of her age.

ROBERT: So I should hope.

EVAN: You ought to meet some of them. Little brutes. They ought to be kept in cages. Have some more whisky?

ROBERT: Thank you, no. (*Sits down.*) I must say, I didn't think much of the friends Cherry brought down here from time to time. Very second-rate. Perhaps you'll put a stop to all that sort of thing.

EVAN: I wouldn't dream of putting a stop to anything. Cherry's private life is entirely her own affair.

ROBERT'S *expression is a study.*

How long have you known the family?

ROBERT: Getting on for fifteen years. They came to live down here when Stella's husband retired from the Navy. I knew both the children as youngsters. Taught your Cherry how to sail. She was always a tom-boy.

EVAN: She's a tom-boy still. That sort of nature, you know. Happy anywhere. Stick her in Holloway gaol and she'd settle down. It makes it all very easy for me. (*He wanders to hatch-window, and looks out.*)

ROBERT *moves to table L. Looks at whisky bottle.*

ROBERT (*gloomily*): Are you going to be down here for long?

EVAN: For life, I should imagine. I've never seen a place I liked better.

ROBERT: Oh! Well, I'd better warn you, houses are extremely hard to find in these parts.

EVAN: What's wrong with this one?

ROBERT: This one happens to belong to your mother-in-law.

EVAN: That's all right. We can all live here together. An enchanting prospect.

ROBERT (*to fire*): Perhaps she wouldn't think so. And, anyway, a young couple should have a place to themselves.

EVAN (*turning round from hatch*): I disagree. And any place run by Cherry would be a shambles in five minutes. You should have seen her flat in London. Positive pigsty. I spent a night there once. Never again.

CHERRY *and* STELLA *enter*. STELLA *carrying sheets and blankets.*

STELLA: Hello, Bob. Just in time for a drink. Have you introduced yourselves?

ROBERT: Yes.

CHERRY (*she goes up to* ROBERT *and kisses him*): Hullo, sweetheart.

STELLA, *intuitive, realises that the encounter between* EVAN *and* ROBERT *has not gone too well.*

EVAN: It's his whisky we've been drinking. And there's only about two inches left in the bottle. I'd have had more respect for it if I'd known.

STELLA: What's happened to the other two bottles?

42

EVAN: Upstairs, beside my bed.

ROBERT *looks disgusted, and* STELLA *sees the look.*

STELLA (*hurriedly*): You must take Evan out sailing in your boat, Bob, dear. Cherry tells me he's crazy to fish. Isn't that so, Evan?

EVAN (*firmly*): Quite correct. I intend to go fishing every day. Without fail. Wet or fine. "Routes."

STELLA *frowns at him, and begins to speak very quickly.*

STELLA: The scenery is wonderful, you know, all round this coast. Some people prefer the North, but I always think it's far too bare and wind-swept. Here we have so many little bays, and lovely valleys, and wild flowers, and then there are always the gulls wheeling about at the mouth of the harbour. Perfect for painting.

CHERRY: But Mother, darling, Evan doesn't paint landscape.

STELLA: Doesn't he? How stupid of me. What do you paint, Evan?

EVAN: The female figure in undress.

STELLA: Ah! Nudes, of course. Wonderful in a gallery, but out of place in a room like this, I always think.

She is rather losing her head.

EVAN: I entirely agree with you. There is nothing quite so unattractive as the average naked woman. I paint exclusively for galleries. And my prices are exorbitant. What are you doing with all those sheets?

He takes them from her.

STELLA: I'm taking them to your divan in the attic. *Not* intuition this time. Cherry's orders.

She looks at him rather severely.

EVAN: I'm sorry to be a nuisance. Do you mind?

STELLA (*gaily*): Mind? Why should I mind? It's not my honeymoon.

Perhaps that whisky did go a little to her head.

ROBERT (*out of his depth, and disapproving of everyone*): Well, I must be getting along.

STELLA (*relieved*): Must you? Oh, don't go. It's quite early yet. Evan, would you like to make your own bed?

EVAN: I always have done.

He turns with sheets and blankets, and walks rather solemnly up the steps to the studio. CHERRY *with a wink at* STELLA, *follows him.*

CHERRY: I'll give you a hand, for all that. Good night, Robert.

They go up to studio.

ROBERT (*to* CHERRY): Good night, Cherry.

STELLA (*moving to fireplace: rather anxious*): Charming, don't you think?

ROBERT: Cherry's husband? I prefer to reserve my opinion.

STELLA (*chastened*): I know that voice. That means you dislike him.

ROBERT: He's had a good whack at my whisky, anyway.

STELLA: Was it really your whisky? How sweet of you, Bob.

She gives him a wonderful smile, which is too much for him.

ROBERT: Well, I promised you, didn't I?

STELLA: Yes, but I know how difficult it is. You shouldn't have bothered.

ROBERT: Now look here, Stella. I want you to promise me something in return. And that is not to go running round wearing yourself out after those two. Let them look after themselves. They're prefectly capable of it.

STELLA: But I love doing it.

ROBERT: That's all very fat and fine. But I know that artistic type. He'll just dig himself in here, probably drink you out of house and home, throw off a lot of moody nonsense, and you'll be the one to suffer from it.

STELLA (*moves around tidying things*): I think you're being very unfair to Evan. You can't possibly judge him in that way after seeing him for two minutes. Besides, this is only a holiday. Cherry tells me he had some wonderful offer from New York only the other day. They're bound to do a lot of travelling.

ROBERT (*following* STELLA *about*): H'm. He told me just now he was going to settle here for life.

STELLA (*interested*): Did he? I couldn't be more pleased.

She tidies the glasses on the tray and empties an ashtray.

I must go and change, and see about the supper. Are you sure you won't stay? Hot lobster, you know. And plenty of it.

ROBERT: No, my dear, thank you very much. There's a meeting of the Harbour Board, and I'm late already. Stella!

STELLA: Yes?

ROBERT: If Cherry and that fellow do decide to live here, and make it their home, indefinitely, and you get fed up with them, you know what to do, don't you?

STELLA: Tell me. (*She knows what he is going to say.*)

ROBERT: There's a house at the top of the hill that's been crying out for you to take charge of it for a very long while.

STELLA (*gently*): Dear Bob.

ROBERT: All right. I won't bore you with the old story now. But you know what I mean, don't you?

STELLA: I do.

ROBERT: It holds good, this day and for ever more.

STELLA: Bless you.

ROBERT (*going out of hatch*): Good night, my dear.

STELLA: Good night, Bob.

She watches him a moment from hatch, then turns, straightens things, pats a cushion or two, looks up at studio door, and goes off L., humming a tune. As she does so, CHERRY *pokes her head from studio.*

CHERRY: Has he gone?

STELLA (*from door L.*): Who—Robert? Yes—why?

CHERRY: Evan wants to know if you had "routes"?

STELLA (*from hall*): Tell Evan to mind his own business!

CHERRY *laughs, comes down in to living-room, throws log on to smouldering fire, and lights a cigarette. EVAN comes down after a moment.*

EVAN: Where's she gone?

CHERRY: Mother? To mix the salad, I suppose, and look at the lobster. Also to drape herself in what she calls a tea-gown. She's very old-fashioned, you know. The war didn't alter her a scrap. A lot of old trouts down here just leapt at the chance of getting into some sort of uniform and throwing their weight about, but Mother remained serene and feminine throughout, rolling band-ages, packing food parcels, and wiping the grubby noses of little bombed-out Plymouth children. Of course, she's thrilled with your arrival. You wait till you see the supper, and all for your benefit. She has bread and butter and a cup of tea when she's alone.

EVAN (*sitting down to piano*): Cup of tea? That's how you described her, didn't you?

CHERRY: Yes; rather apt, don't you think.

EVAN *laughs and doesn't answer.*

Go on. Try out the old piano. It's probably very tinny. Nobody ever plays on it.

EVAN *begins to play very softly "At Seventeen" from the "Maid of the Mountains." The sun is setting through the windows.*

(*Comes and stands by him.*) The tuner comes from Exeter every quarter, and tells Mother she must not put flowers on the piano, and she smiles sweetly at him, and promises never to again, and then puts them back again

47

as soon as he's out of the house. What's that you're playing? I've never heard it.

EVAN: Not your vintage. Daly's, 1918.

CHERRY: Heaven's above! Whatever age were you?

EVAN: Oh, rising nine. I wore my first Eton jacket, and was taken by my mother, in the front row of the stalls. She wore a gardenia in her hair, and I bought her a box of chocolates for half a crown.

CHERRY: How very precocious of you.

EVAN: I was a very precocious little boy.

He switches from "At Seventeen" to the waltz song, "Love will find a way."

CHERRY: It's news to me that you can play this sort of stuff at all. I thought you despised it.

EVAN: Did you? But then, you know very little about me, one way and another.

CHERRY: Think so?

STELLA comes in. She is wearing a very becoming tea-gown and she has put a clip in her hair.

STELLA: Oh! my favourite song. "The Maid of the Mountains." How did you know?

EVAN: Intuition. Have some more whisky.

STELLA (*happily*): Bless you. How it takes me back! (*Hums, pours herself a small drink.*)

CHERRY (*laughing*): Now she'll be well away. (*To STELLA*) Darling, you are so *incredibly* sentimental.

48

STELLA: I'm not sentimental. I'm romantic. There's all the difference in the world between the two. Isn't there, Evan? (*She sits on sofa.*)

EVAN: Between romance and sentiment? Not a jot of difference. I wallow in both.

CHERRY: Oh! You liar. You're the cynic of all time.

EVAN: So *you* think. But I'm Jekyll and Hyde. You only know Hyde.

He slips into "Delia" from the "Merry Widow."

CHERRY: You'll have Mother in tears in a minute, and then we shan't get any supper. Darling, you look very sweet, and you smell heavenly. But then you always do. I'll wash my hands and powder my nose, but I needn't change, need I?

STELLA: Not if you don't want to.

EVAN (*from piano, to* CHERRY): Slut!

CHERRY *makes a face at him and exits L.*

STELLA (*rather shocked*): Is that the usual way for bridegrooms to address their brides?

EVAN: When they have brides like Cherry—yes. (*He laughs at her.*) That's a lovely colour you're wearing.

STELLA (*looking down at dress*): It's years old and very faded. But I always change for supper, even when I'm alone. One of my rules. (*She gets up and goes to window.*)

EVAN: Like missionaries in New Guinea. Stops them from going native. You're very paintable.

49

STELLA: Thank you. I thought you only painted nudes.

EVAN: That's when I lack other inspiration. (*Ceases playing.*)

STELLA: Oh! don't stop. I do so love it. Play the song from the "Maid of the Mountains" again. I heard you from upstairs.

EVAN *begins "At Seventeen" again.*

Yes, that's the one. Thorpe Bates, wasn't it? And José Collins. I went on my birthday. I remember wearing a bright pink frock, and crying all through the last act.

EVAN: Who were you crying for? The artist in your life, or the flag-lieutenant?

STELLA: For neither. I was crying for Thorpe Bates.

EVAN *laughs at her from the piano.*

I don't know how you know the song, anyway. You must have been a child in arms at the time.

She moves down to piano, and leans upon it.

EVAN: A child perhaps. But not in arms. A preparatory school was doing its best to drive the iron into my romantic soul. But it didn't succeed.

STELLA: I'm glad.

EVAN: Glad? What about?

STELLA: Glad that it didn't succeed. If it had, you probably wouldn't be playing the piano to me now. When my Jimmy went away to school, at the pitiful age of eight and a quarter, I went about wearing dark glasses for a week. If anyone spoke to me I burst into tears. He returned changed beyond recognition. I don't think I ever quite got over that.

EVAN: He'll come back again one day, you know. They always do. Like a homing pigeon.

STELLA: Oh, if he wants anything, of course. But that's not really what I mean.

EVAN: No. I know it isn't.

Pause as EVAN *continues playing.*

STELLA: Is your mother living?

EVAN: No. She died of pneumonia when I was just fourteen. The iron did enter my soul then—for many years.

STELLA (*gently*): Poor little boy.

EVAN: Not poor little boy. Unpleasant little bastard.

STELLA: Things, and people, hurt us so much when we are young, don't they? And then, as we grow older, the pain seems to flatten out, it doesn't mean the same. No more crying into pillows. No more stabs below the heart.

EVAN *has reached the last few bars of the song, and as he plays it, he sings the words half-consciously, and* STELLA *hums them, too.*

"But when he thought he'd passed love,
   'Twas then he met his last love,
    And he loved her as he'd never loved before."

The ship's bell, ringing shrilly from the hall, gives warning of supper.

STELLA (*waving glass*): Supper. Cherry's getting hungry.

EVAN (*smiling at her*): To hell with supper!

He breaks into "Love will find a way" in rather more rapid time, and STELLA, *rising, goes to draw curtains and light lamps, humming the tune as she does so.*

51

EVAN *begins to hum as well, and* STELLA, *after drawing the curtains, comes and stands behind him at the piano. They are both singing riotously and happily as* CHERRY *enters from hall R. ringing the bell loudly.*

CHERRY (*with a hopeless gesture*): Well! For God's sake.

CURTAIN

ACT 2

The Studio. Two months later. Afternoon. This room is hard to describe, and I think is best left to the ingenuity of the designer. Originally an attic, it should have a long, low appearance, with sloping walls and a skylight. R. centre is a swing-door, hooked back against the wall, which has a ten-foot drop to the slip below, reached by a ladder. Back L. is the door to the steps of living-room, and R. a small open hearth, with L. down-stage, a divan, a chair, perhaps a screen. The walls are distempered, one or two good rugs on the floor. Canvases are stacked against the wall, and there is a small table with the usual studio litter—paints, brushes, etc.

MRS. TUCKET, acting as a model, is kneeling on the floor, a shawl round her shoulders. EVAN stands at his easel L. forward of the hooked-back door, and is intent on a tricky piece of work upon MRS. TUCKET's cheekbone.

EVAN (*in the voice of one who has not heard a word of previous conversation*): And after his eleventh operation—what did your husband do then?

MRS. T.: He rallied for a few months, Mr. Davies, but he was never fit for what you might call hard work, not after they removed the stone. As large as a pigeon's egg, it was. The surgeon said he'd never seen anything like it, and he'd been doing similar operations for thirty years. No wonder my poor Tom had gone clean off his food.

EVAN (*brush between his teeth*): No wonder at all.

MRS. T.: It was the eating nothing that worried me in the first place, because Tom was always one for his dinner. Never would say no to an egg-and-ham pasty. But he got so thin and drawn, with his hand always to his side, and he couldn't rest at nights. Why, Mr. Davies, I've had him sitting up in the bed with his knees drawn right up to his chin—he said he felt the pain less that way. And sweat—I've never seen a horse sweat like he did. He'd stream buckets.

EVAN, *with brush still between his teeth, makes the appropriate sympathetic noises.*

But it was the bath up at the Infirmary that finished him in the end. He was taken bad one dinner-time, and doctor called him up there for observation. Sister should have known better, the shock of the water, and him not being used to it. He said to the nurse as she led him up to it, "I'll die if you put me into that," he said. And die he did.

EVAN (*very slowly, as he carefully touches cheekbone*): And die he did.

MRS. T.: A lovely husband he made me, Mr. Davies. A lovely husband. Never an angry word. And we were sweethearts right up to the end. That's what marriage ought to be, as I was saying to Mrs. Martyn only this morning as we were making the beds.

EVAN (*preoccupied with painting*): U'm. U'm.

MRS. T.: Keep courting, Mrs. Martyn, I said. That's the answer to a happy marriage. From the time you come down the aisle after your wedding, to the time you're carried up it feet first at your funeral, keep courting.

Pause.

EVAN: You must have led a very exhausting life one way and another.

MRS. T.: Get along. I don't feel a day more than twenty-five. I dare say I'm as young in heart as your Miss Cherry, and twice as active.

EVAN: That wouldn't be difficult.

MRS. T.: Bless her dear heart. She's a handsome maid.

EVAN (*steps back looking at his work*): A handsome maid.

MRS. T.: But I tell you one thing, Mr. Davies. Though she is your wife and a fine young woman, she'll never be as good-looking as her mother.

MRS. TUCKET *pauses for confirmation of this, but* EVAN *does not answer.*

I've known Mrs. Martyn for getting on twelve years, ever since I came down here to live, and she's prettier now than she's ever been. Young and gay, and full of life. It's having you and Miss Cherry here to live that's done it. She's looked ten years younger and a different woman ever since you came, as I was saying to my daughter only yesterday. Well, it stands to reason, doesn't it? 'Tisn't natural for a woman to live alone, especially when she's someone like Mrs. Martyn.

EVAN: Why Mrs. Martyn in particular?

MRS. T.: Because she's the giving kind. The kind that spend themselves for their men-folk. And they're the kind that love the longest.

Pause.

You never knew the Commander, did you?

55

EVAN: The Commander?

MRS. T.: Commander Martyn, Miss Cherry's father.

EVAN: No.

MRS. T.: Nice gentleman, but peaky. Always ailing. Mr. Jimmy takes after him. I thought so last time he was on leave. You'll see. Mrs. Martyn will wear herself out for him in the end, just as she did for the Commander.

Pause.

EVAN: Well—I think that's probably all for to-day, Mrs. Tucket.

MRS. T.: You mean you're finished with me?

EVAN: Yes. We've had the best of the light.

EVAN *turns and begins to clean his palette and brushes, etc.* MRS. TUCKET *gets up from floor, rubbing herself. She was getting a bit stiff.*

MRS. T.: Can I take a peep?

EVAN: Sure. Go ahead.

MRS. T. (*walking round to easel*): Oh! My dear life.

EVAN: Like it?

MRS. T.: Handsome. A proper job. What you'd call a speaking likeness.

EVAN: Glad you think so.

MRS. T.: Will this be hung in a London gallery, Mr. Davies?

EVAN: I dare say.

MRS. T.: With strangers coming in to look at it?

EVAN: Hundreds. Probably have to have policemen to keep back the crowds.

MRS. T.: Did you ever!

CHERRY *whistles from outside swing-door, and her head bobs up from the ladder. She climbs into the studio. Dressed in sailing trousers and smock; hair untidy.*

CHERRY: Lost by half a minute. That bloody Ruby caught a puff of wind from the south just as we were coming up to the Club, sailed in under our lee, and got the gun. I only hope everybody heard our language. . . . Well, how's it going?

EVAN: Fine. Just packing up.

MRS. T.: Oh, Miss Cherry, come and look at my portrait, do. Proper stylish, it is.

CHERRY (*coming and standing beside easel*): Ah, then you have taken away those shadows, after all.

EVAN (*standing beside her*): Yes, it's made a difference, hasn't it?

CHERRY: Much better. That's a nice piece of modelling on the cheekbone.

EVAN: Been working on that just now.

CHERRY: It's damn good.

EVAN: H'm. Not bad. I shall have to do something about her left eye. It's all over the shop.

MRS. T. (*indignant*): What's wrong with my left eye? I've never worn glasses yet.

CHERRY: Don't worry, Mrs. Tucket. I'll see he doesn't spoil your beauty for you.

MRS. T.: He'd better not! If he did, there's plenty would want to know the reason why. Isn't that so, Miss Cherry? (*Winks knowingly at* CHERRY.)

CHERRY (*laughing, sits on divan*): So they tell me. You'd better watch out, you know, Evan, or you'll get your head bashed in. Mrs. Tucket's old boy-friend on the Ferry doesn't approve of her sitting for her portrait.

EVAN: Sorry about that. You didn't tell me, Mrs. Tucket. I thought you had no other follower but myself.

MRS. T. (*delighted*): Get along. . . . Why, yes, Mr. Davies. Joe on the Ferry has courted me steady for five years now, but he never gets anywhere. You're all skin and bone, Joe, I tell him. You'd never keep anyone warm on a winter's night! (*She turns towards the door.*) Do you think there's anything more I can do for your mother, Miss Cherry?

CHERRY: I shouldn't think so, Mrs. Tucket. She washed up after lunch, didn't she, and turned out my room? I'd get along back home to my tea, if I were you.

MRS. T.: See you in the morning, then. And I'll be free again at two o'clock for you, Mr. Davies, if that's all right by Mrs. Martyn. 'Tis a real pleasure to do it, and you're welcome any time. Good afternoon.

She exits down to living-room.

CHERRY (*laughing, lighting cigarette*): Garrulous old bitch.

Pause.

EVAN (*still cleaning his palette*): Why the devil didn't she tell me that coming up here to sit took her off household chores?

58

CHERRY: Only too delighted to get out of them, I expect.

EVAN: Has this been going on all the time she's been sitting for me?

CHERRY: Has what been going on?

EVAN: Stella washing up, and doing the things Mrs. Tucket normally does.

CHERRY: Of course. What of it. Mother doesn't mind.

Pause.

EVAN: Do you ever offer to help?

CHERRY: Good God, no. I'd be terribly in the way.

EVAN: At least you could have cleaned out your own room.

CHERRY: I made my bed! Anyway, I didn't get up till half-past twelve, and I've been sailing all the afternoon. (*She yawns, stretches herself, runs hand through hair.*)

EVAN: What do you suppose she's doing now?

CHERRY: Mother? Washing all the hair-brushes, I imagine. I saw rows of them laid out on her balcony above just now. (*Gets up, potters round the studio, looking at the canvasses against the wall.*) I'm sorry you didn't·go on with that head of young Brian. It was so sensitive.

EVAN: The child was too restless. Couldn't keep him still a minute.

He has his back to CHERRY. *She pulls out a canvas from the back. Gives a cry of surprise.*

CHERRY: Oh! But, Evan . . . this is wonderful. When did you do it?

EVAN (*whips round quickly*): What have you got there?

CHERRY: Why—this head of Mother.

EVAN: Put it down.

CHERRY: What for? What's the matter?

EVAN (*he is very angry*): Give it to me.

CHERRY (*replacing canvas against wall*): How funny you
are. Why the awful secrecy? (*She stares at him, quite
bewildered, then her face suddenly clears.*) Oh! I know.
You sly old thing. You were doing it as a surprise for
my birthday. Was that it?

EVAN (*after a pause*): Yes.

CHERRY: I'm terribly sorry I spoilt the fun. I promise I
won't look again. But how very exciting, and what a
lovely idea. When do you work on it? Mother hasn't said
a word.

EVAN: She doesn't know.

CHERRY: Doesn't know? What on earth do you mean?

EVAN (*impatient*): She hasn't sat for it. I've been doing it
from memory. Working on it in the early mornings.

CHERRY: But how wonderful! Now I know why you asked
for an alarm clock up here. (*Seizes clock by divan.*)
Let's look. Yes! It's set for a quarter to six. I never
thought anything on earth would get you up with the
sun! You wily old thing. Well, if it turns out to be the
picture of all time, it will be worth it. How exciting for
Mother, too. She's going to get the thrill of her life.

EVAN (*edgy*): Oh! For God's sake . . .

CHERRY (*surprised*): Don't be scratchy. . . . You know how pleased she'll be. (*Pause.*) Well, I must change if I'm going to the pictures with Pam Tremayne. Are you coming?

EVAN: No.

CHERRY: Come on. Do you good. It's Ingrid Bergman, and you know you like her.

EVAN: I don't. She bores me stiff.

As he says this, STELLA *comes in at door from living-room, carrying* EVAN's *hair-brushes, also armful of logs.*

STELLA: Who bores you stiff?

She is wearing a thin tweed skirt, and a camel-hair jumper. Rather flushed from carrying logs, but young and gay.

EVAN (*angry at her full hands*): What *are* you doing? I've told you about this before. (*He seizes logs from her and throws them into the hearth.*)

STELLA: They're not heavy.

She sees expression on his face and turns enquiringly to CHERRY, *who shrugs her shoulder.*

What are you two arguing about?

CHERRY: Pam and I are going to the pictures. I'm trying to persuade Evan to come with us.

STELLA: Oh, yes . . . fun. Go with them, Evan.

EVAN: I don't want to.

STELLA: You'd enjoy it.

EVAN: I would not. (*He is very busy stacking his brushes and paints.*)

CHERRY: Never nag a man into doing something he doesn't want to do. I've learnt that much from marriage, if nothing else. Did you mend my trousers, darling?

STELLA: Yes, they're on your bed.

CHERRY: Can I borrow your scarf? The new one?

STELLA: Of course.

CHERRY: Don't wait supper. We shall probably do a pub-crawl afterwards and end up at the White Hart. Well, take care of yourselves. (*Makes a face at EVAN's back. Smiles at STELLA.*) Pamper him!

CHERRY exits L. EVAN continues with his back to STELLA. She comes forward, having put his brushes on a side table.

STELLA (*after a pause*): You should have gone with her.

EVAN: Why?

STELLA: It would have made her so happy.

EVAN: I've often told you I'm not the sort who goes round making other people happy. Never have been, and never will be.

There is another pause. STELLA kneels to see to fire.

STELLA: Sometimes I get worried about you and Cherry.

EVAN: Why?

STELLA: I don't know. . . . You're both so casual. I suppose I'm old-fashioned, but it all seems so different from when I was young and newly-married.

EVAN: It is different.

STELLA: You know—it's different, too, having you both here, from what I thought it would be. You don't do things together, the way I had imagined. Cherry goes off sailing on her own, or to the cinema with a friend, as she is doing to-night—and you either paint here all day, or play the piano, or sit and talk to me. I wonder if all modern marriages are so lacking in—— (*Pauses.*)

EVAN: Lacking in what?

STELLA: Well—romance, to put it bluntly.

EVAN: Are you thinking of your gold-braided past?

STELLA: No—not exactly. I don't know what I'm thinking of. Perhaps what I would feel if I were Cherry. (*She gets up, moves L.*)

EVAN: What would you feel?

STELLA: Oh, but I'd want to share every moment with my husband. I'd want to be with him all the time. Whether it was in a boat, or in a studio, or anywhere—it wouldn't matter, just as long as we were together. I wouldn't really have a mind of my own at all. (*Pause.*) Perhaps the war has killed that sort of instinct. I don't pretend to understand what goes on in Cherry's mind. (*She opens cigarette box. Sees that it is empty.*) You need more cigarettes. I got you some this morning, but I'm afraid not the kind you like best. They hadn't anything else. (*Fills box, picks up whisky decanter, which is nearly full.*) You're being very good with this. I filled it up last week, and it's only gone down one inch. What's happened to you?

EVAN: Haven't felt like whisky.

STELLA: Would you rather have gin instead?

EVAN: No, I don't want anything.

STELLA (*happy*): It's that swim before breakfast that's done it. It's very good for you. I time myself by you every morning. When I hear you dive off the slip into the harbour I say to myself, "Half-past eight. There's Evan. Time to get out of bed."

EVAN (*smiling*): Do you?

CHERRY *calls up from below,* "I'm off." STELLA *answers,* "Goodbye, darling. Have a good time."

STELLA (*after pause*): I still think you ought to have gone with her.

He doesn't answer. She sits on divan, looks about the room, puts on her glasses, and reaches for workbox.

I'm so glad you like this room, and that you're happy here. You've no idea what fun it was getting it ready for you. And very anxious-making, too, because I wasn't sure if you'd like it or not. I was so afraid you might be temperamental, and want to paint in the kitchen or something. (*Pause.*) I used to sit up here by myself sometimes after the children went to school. Of course, it wasn't furnished or anything, but I had a funny old table, and used to mend all the linen here on wet afternoons. It was still and peaceful. I can remember sitting for hours, listening to the water coming up on to the slip below, and dreaming—dreaming about nothing at all. (*She smiles, happy and reminiscent.*)

EVAN: Don't move.

STELLA (*sub-conscious hand to tidy hair*): What's the matter?

EVAN: Keep just as you were. Please. (*He goes to the wall, picks up canvas with its face to wall, and puts it upon the easel. Stands with his arms folded, and his eyes nearly closed, staring at it.*) I *was* right. That little line at the corner of your mouth does turn inward. (*He seizes palette and brush in a frenzy.*)

STELLA: What are you talking about?

EVAN: Be quiet.

She sits quite still, rather unnerved, while he works in silence.

STELLA: How long do I have to go on sitting like this?

EVAN: For as long as I tell you.

STELLA: Evan dear, tell me what it's all about. Am I a substitute for Mrs. Tucket?

EVAN: No, darling.

He is intent on the work, and probably unconscious that he has called her "darling." But she looks up, a little anxious, a little puzzled. Pause.

STELLA: Evan . . . I really came up here to talk to you about quite a lot of things.

EVAN: What sort of things?

STELLA: Well—the future. What you're going to do. Your and Cherry's plans.

EVAN: I never make plans.

STELLA: That offer from America. Cherry told me you had another letter about it only yesterday. Will you go?

EVAN: God, no!

65

STELLA: Why not?

EVAN: Why should I go to America when I'm happy here?

STELLA: Cherry might like it. You might like it, too. It might be awfully good for you both.

EVAN: Do you want to get rid of us, or what?

STELLA (*upset*): Oh, no . . . no . . .

EVAN: Stop talking, then, and don't move your head. (*He paints intently for a moment, and then steps back, stares at canvas, smiles, and lays down palette. Lights a cigarette.*) There! Finished! If I never paint another picture for the rest of my life, it won't matter a damn. I've done what I wanted to do. I've done something good.

STELLA (*hesitating*): Can I see?

EVAN (*looks at her*): If you want to.

STELLA *gets up from divan, and goes and stands by easel. They neither of them speak. There is a long pause, as* STELLA *looks at the portrait, and as she does so, her face changes, becomes pensive, wistful, as though looking at the portrait she was looking at herself for the first time. Tears come into her eyes. She stands a moment longer, then goes to the door, her back turned to* EVAN.

Where are you going?

STELLA: To my room.

EVAN: Why?

STELLA (*turning and facing him*): Because I don't want you to see me cry.

They stand looking at each other for a moment, and then from below we can hear the voice of ROBERT

HANSON *calling,* "Stella? Stella?" ROBERT *calls* "Stella?" *again, obviously from the foot of the steps in living-room.* STELLA *goes and sits again on divan with work-basket.*

Hullo, Bob. I'm up here, in the studio.

EVAN *gives her one look, then swiftly takes down canvas and places it against wall, replacing it with canvas of* MRS. TUCKET. *We hear* ROBERT *coming up the steps, and* STELLA *bends over her work basket.*

ROBERT (*entering door*): Hullo. Hullo. I called, but getting no answer, thought everyone must be out.

STELLA: Evan was just showing me Mrs. Tucket's portrait. It's very good indeed.

ROBERT: Oh, splendid. Am I permitted to look?

EVAN (*quietly*): Of course.

ROBERT (*goes and stands by easel. After pause*): Yes . . . Well, you'd know it was Mrs. Tucket all right . . .

STELLA: And that's what I'd call a masterpiece of under-statement. (*To* EVAN) He means he likes it.

EVAN: I'm glad.

ROBERT: Going to show it in New York, I suppose?

EVAN: What makes you think I'd show it in New York?

ROBERT: Sort of thing that would appeal to them, wouldn't it? Local colour and all that. Besides, think of the dollars you'd bring in.

STELLA (*swiftly*): But Evan isn't going to New York, Bob, so the question doesn't arise.

ROBERT: Oh! I rather gathered from Cherry there'd been some offer or other. Perhaps I got hold of the wrong end of the stick. Where is Cherry, by the way? (*Sits.*)

STELLA: She's gone to the cinema.

ROBERT: All by herself?

STELLA: No, with Pam Tremayne.

ROBERT: It's going to be a filthy evening. She'll get very wet.

STELLA: She's got an oilskin.

There is a pause. The situation, for some reason or other, is rather strained.

ROBERT (*rising*): It's going to blow much harder when the tide returns. There must have been a gale warning. I see they've hoisted the cone. Is Cherry's boat riding to the light anchor only? (*This to* EVAN.)

EVAN: I haven't the least idea.

ROBERT: Oh. Well, if it blows like I think it will, the boat will drag. Something ought to be done about it. You never know what will happen with a September tide, they're damned tricky things.

Nobody says anything.

I've known more damage done at this time of the year than in all the winter months put together. I've put down twenty fathoms on my boat, and she'll ride through anything. (*Pause.*) I remember once—

STELLA (*not very pressing*): Have a drink, Bob?

ROBERT (*crosses to her, glancing at* EVAN): No, I don't think I will. It was pretty fresh sailing outside, and I got

68

very wet. I'm going straight home to change. As a matter of fact, Stella, I really came to ask if you'd care to come up and have dinner with me to-night.

STELLA: Oh! How sweet of you. I'm afraid I can't to-night, Bob. You see, Cherry will come straight home after the cinema and want a hot supper, and, as you know, Mrs. Tucket doesn't come in the evenings. Some other time, I'd love to come. And, anyway, if it's going to be very wet . . .

She listens as rain patters suddenly on skylight.

Ah! Here it comes. (*She says this almost with relief.*) You'd better get home quickly, Bob, before you're soaked through.

ROBERT (*drily*): I also have an oilskin. (*To* EVAN) Don't forget to put down that other anchor. That is, if you know how to.

EVAN: I think I do.

ROBERT: H'm. Well, I hope Cherry enjoys her cinema. Don't bother to come down, Stella, I can let myself out.

He exits, leaving behind him an aura of disapproval.

STELLA (*whispering*): He's on a hard chair.

EVAN (*also whispering*): What's a hard chair?

STELLA (*still whispering*): My private word for someone who is offended.

Pause. And then the clang of the hatch-door below.

EVAN: He was right about the gale. It is going to blow. Badly.

He unhooks door to slip, and fastens it. The room has grown suddenly very dark. The rain patters down heavily on skylight.

EVAN: Is it "routes" to tell fibs to Robert?

STELLA: Tell fibs?

EVAN: Yes. First you said I was showing you Mrs. Tucket's picture, and then you said you couldn't have dinner with him because you had to get a hot supper for Cherry. You know Cherry is having supper at the White Hart.

STELLA: I'd forgotten.

EVAN: Had you?

STELLA (*in a small voice*): No.

> EVAN *laughs; reaches for a pair of seaboots in corner.*

What are you going to do?

EVAN: Cope with that anchor while I can still see.

STELLA: Be careful. You're not very expert, remember. What do you want for supper?

> EVAN *smiles. Reaches for his coat.*

EVAN: Ever tasted omelette *à la esperanza?*

STELLA: No, what is it?

EVAN: Spanish—with a dash of Portuguese. I learnt how to make them in Teneriffe. You shall have one to-night. Here, in the studio. Got any burgundy?

STELLA: Nuits St. Georges. One bottle.

EVAN: We'll have that, too. I'll light the fire when I've put down that anchor, and you shall bring up the burgundy and put it to warm. Also bring a frying-pan, half a dozen eggs, chives, and some olive oil. Don't forget the olive oil. It's very important.

STELLA: You ask for the impossible.

EVAN: You've never refused the impossible—yet.

STELLA *laughs. She is gay once more, her tears forgotten.*

One other thing. You haven't worn that green dress lately. Wear it to-night.

STELLA: How ridiculous you are. Are we celebrating something?

EVAN: But of course. It's a very great occasion. We're celebrating the fact that you and I have never had supper alone together before.

He exits down to living-room, STELLA patting his shoulder with a laugh. She listens a moment, then goes to hooked-door, and opens it a few inches.

STELLA: Evan?

EVAN (*from the slip*): Hullo?

STELLA: Be careful.

EVAN gives answering shout, and STELLA shuts the door. She turns back into the studio, and after a moment, goes rather furtively to canvas against the wall, and puts it once more upon the easel. She turns very slowly to look at herself in the mirror hanging on the wall.

CURTAIN

(The curtain remains down a few moments only, to show passing of time.)

71

*The same. The evening. Candlesticks, alight, stand on
the table that has been dragged into the centre of the
studio. There are also lighted candles on the small table
by divan. Another, perhaps, stuck in a saucer by painting table. The lamp is also lit. So is the fire.*

STELLA, *changed into her tea-gown, is standing by the
centre table mixing the salad.* EVAN, *kneeling by the fire,
holds a frying-pan over the logs, and is stirring the con-
tents.*

STELLA: The salad's mixed. Can I do anything else for you?

EVAN: You can shut your eyes and pray. This is my finest
hour. Never have so many eggs been smashed into so
much olive oil with apparently so little result. Fetch me
the pepper and salt.

STELLA (*bringing them*): It smells very good. (*She bends
over him.*)

EVAN: So do you. What is it?

STELLA: White Lilac. The last of a very small bottle.

EVAN: Take yourself away. I can't concentrate. Everything
depends upon the next few seconds.

STELLA *laughs and moves back to table.*

They begin to stir. . . . They begin to come to life.
. . . They begin to do what they ought to have done
five minutes ago. Pray God I haven't lost my cunning.

72

STELLA: We can always fall back on the corned beef if it's a failure.

EVAN: It won't be a failure. Corned beef my eye! Have you no soul, woman? Got the plates ready?

STELLA (*fetching plates*): This is terribly exciting. Like eating one's first oyster.

EVAN: Which is invariably disappointing, like everything else in life, when eaten too young. (*He rises from fire, frying-pan in hand, and slices some of the omelette on to* STELLA's *plate and the rest on to his own.*) If you're disappointed in this, it either means you have a jaded palate or your eggs were rotten.

STELLA (*sits down; bends over plate, sniffs*): It looks lovely.

EVAN *puts down pan, reaches for the bottle of wine that has been warming by the fire, uncorks it and pours out a glass for himself and* STELLA.

EVAN: *Vous êtes servie, madame. Bon appetit.*

STELLA: *Asseyez vous. Sur le* floor.

They begin to eat, and then look at each other.

EVAN (*mouth full*): H'm (*Meaning "All right?"*)

STELLA (*mouth full*): H'm (*Meaning "It is"*)

EVAN: Could have done with just one minute longer in the pan, and a few more chives.

STELLA: I don't agree. It's perfect as it is. Any longer in the pan and it would have been overdone.

EVAN: I'm an artist, you see. In cooking, as in other things. And an artist is never satisfied with his work. It could always be just that much better.

73

STELLA: What about my portrait? Aren't you satisfied with that?

EVAN (*looking at her*): I was—about three hours ago. Not any longer. Not when I see you in that dress.

STELLA (*matter of fact*): I told you before, it's a very old dress. Have some salad.

EVAN (*helps himself*): Down to earth and practical, aren't you?

STELLA: Why not? All my clothes are years old. I bought this one originally in case James and I were ever asked to Buckingham Palace. We never were.

EVAN: Did you mind?

STELLA (*looking at him over the glass; pretending*): Yes.

EVAN (*laughs*): And now, instead of dining with the highest in the land, the dress is reduced to supper in a studio with an inarticulate artist over an underdone omelette. But you needn't spill the omelette down the dress. (*He jumps up and dabs at the spot on her dress with his table napkin.*)

STELLA: Oh! How clumsy of me.

EVAN: Very. (*Resumes his seat and goes on eating.*)

STELLA: What are you going to do with it?

EVAN: Do with what?

STELLA: With my portrait.

EVAN: I don't know. What do you suggest I do with it?

STELLA: Put it away with its face to the wall, in the darkest cupboard you can find, where no one will ever see it.

EVAN (*pause*): I'm sorry. I thought you liked it.

STELLA: I do. That's why I want you to put it away.

She drinks her wine. EVAN *watches her.*

EVAN: Tell me something.

STELLA: Yes?

EVAN: Why did it make you cry?

She doesn't answer for a moment.

STELLA: I cry very easily. I thought you knew that. It's one of the first signs of advancing middle age.

EVAN: Nonsense. And, anyway, you haven't answered my question.

STELLA (*breaking some bread*): It isn't an easy one to answer, Evan. I think perhaps that I was reminded, rather suddenly and unexpectedly, of all the things that used to be. Or perhaps it would be more truthful to say—of all the things that might have been.

EVAN: Is that what the portrait said to you?

STELLA (*after pause*): Yes.

EVAN: It didn't say that when I was working on it.

STELLA: What did it say to you?

EVAN: It told me I wasn't painting the past at all. Only the present. Only the things that are.

STELLA (*smiling a little wistfully*): You're really very sweet.

A pause. EVAN *finishes his omelette.*

75

EVAN: Nothing is ever lost, you know. Whatever you wanted once and had, or didn't have; whatever made you happy, or whatever made you sad—it's all there in your eyes, in those little lines on your forehead, in that curve at the corner of your mouth. The things themselves are forgotten. When I worked on that portrait, I wasn't painting a Stella of yesterday, or ten, twenty years ago. They don't matter any more. They've merged into the final, complete person that you are now. The Stella of to-day.

STELLA: Is anybody ever final and complete?

EVAN: I think so. I think everyone reaches a moment when he or she stands tiptoe on the point of balance, and time stands still for about forty seconds. A man will never do better work than he can do in those metaphorical forty seconds, and a woman will never look lovelier. They are both, for the first and last and only time in their lives, their complete selves. Then the point of balance over-tips—and the decline sets in.

STELLA: But—how very depressing.

EVAN: Very.

STELLA: And rather above my head.

EVAN: Decidedly. Finish your omelette.

She smiles and eats a moment in silence; then pushes away her plate.

STELLA (*sighing*): It was very good and very filling. The omelette *à la esperanza*. Why do you call it that?

EVAN: *Esperanza* is the Spanish for "Hope." As a matter of fact, I invented the name on the spur of the moment. Have some more Nuits St. Georges. That's not so very bad either. (*He fills her glass.*)

76

STELLA: The last of a good vintage. The last of my pre-war cellar. We're down to the dregs of everything to-night. The wine, my scent; and I don't think I can go on wearing this dress much longer. No more Nuits St. Georges. No more White Lilac. The decline and fall of Stella Martyn. Do you want any coffee?

EVAN: If you don't have to go down and get it.

STELLA: No, it's all here, in a thermos.

She moves to divan, and pours out coffee. He sits watching her, smoking a cigarette.

EVAN: It was wrong what I said just now about the portrait. It isn't the final, complete Stella after all. You've changed, even in the little time we've sat here having supper. The portrait's out of date already.

STELLA: How have I changed? New lines? New grey hairs?

EVAN: Your eyes are darker than they were this afternoon. And there's a little smudge on the right side of your nose I don't remember.

STELLA (*pulling out a handkerchief*): A smut?

EVAN: No, not a smut.

STELLA: That point of balance you were telling me about. I'm overtipping it?

EVAN laughs. He gets up and walks across to where the portrait stands on the easel. STELLA drinks coffee.

EVAN: A few hours ago that was a damn good portrait. Now it isn't good any longer. You're right about putting it away in a dark cupboard.

STELLA: It *is* a good portrait, and the only reason I ask you to put it away in a dark cupboard is because I don't want anyone else to look at it. Come and drink your coffee.

But EVAN *smiles at her. He doesn't move.*

What's the matter?

EVAN: Nothing's the matter. I'm happy, that's all.

STELLA: Why suddenly?

He comes over and takes his cup of coffee.

EVAN: Not suddenly. I've been happy all the evening, but happy at this moment especially because you have the same feeling about the portrait that I have. You see—I don't want anyone else to look at it either.

The atmosphere is a little tense. STELLA *is uncertain, not sure what he means.*

STELLA (*a shade too brightly*): Finish up your coffee. And you've lost a button from your shirt-sleeve. I'll sew it on directly. (*She begins to clear the things from the table. Stacks crocks on to a tray.*) We needn't wash up. Mrs. Tucket can do it in the morning.

EVAN: Give me the tray. I can do this.

STELLA: Just put it in the kitchen, will you? And shut the window. I have a feeling I forgot it.

He goes down steps to living-room with tray. STELLA *picks up work basket which was lying on the divan, and begins to search in it for a button and a needle and thread.* EVAN *comes back, pours out the last of the wine for himself and* STELLA, *moves lamp a little nearer.* STELLA *puts on large pair of tortoise-shell glasses, and, sitting down on divan, close to lamp, threads needle.*

Come here, and I'll do that button for you.

EVAN *kneels beside her and holds out his arm obediently.*

You're very good about your clothes. You need so little doing to them. Cherry's quite hopeless; and when Jimmy is home I seem to be mending things for him all the time. I don't know why it is; and they're both so untidy, too. I suppose I brought them up badly. Come closer. I can't see.

EVAN *kneels nearer to her, so that his face is almost touching her hair. She sews away, quite unconscious.*

EVAN: Looking at you from this distance, I can see a million things where I went wrong in that portrait. There is so much more light in your hair, and you've got less chin that I thought.

STELLA: How you managed any of it, when I never sat for you once, I can't imagine.

EVAN: If you watch a face day after day for two months, and think of very little else, you come in time to know it rather well.

STELLA: I haven't been aware that you were watching me.

EVAN: Haven't you?

STELLA: Now you've made me lose the thread. (*Breaks off old bit.*) Anyway, I still don't know when you found the time to do it. You've been painting Mrs. Tucket and various other people.

EVAN: I've been getting up at half-past five in the morning. Don't you remember remarking on the fact that I always seemed sleepy at lunch? I've lost quite a bit of sleep one way and another.

STELLA: That was very foolish of you.

EVAN: Very foolish.

STELLA: You've torn the stuff below the button. I'll mend that for you to-morrow. I can't see to do it in this light, any more than you could see to do your painting. I'll have to start getting up at five in the morning, too. (*She breaks thread, does up the button, and smiles up at him.*) There. How's that? What about the other one? Shall I have a look and see if that's loose too?

EVAN: No.

He speaks quietly, in a sort of dream, and as though he doesn't know what he is doing he puts up his hand, and takes the glasses from her face, and kisses her. It is done before she realises what has happened. She sits quite still.

STELLA (*after a moment, and in a whisper*): No, no. . . .

EVAN: Yes.

He kisses her once more.

STELLA (*very distressed, pushing him away*): No . . . no.

She gets up from the divan, and turns away from him. EVAN watches her. Rises to his feet.

Why did you do that? Just when we were so happy? You've spoilt everything.

EVAN: What have I spoilt?

STELLA: Our being all together, here in this house. You and I and Cherry. Cherry . . .

She turns and faces him. It is difficult for her, and distressing, to say any more.

EVAN: We needn't bring Cherry into this. She hasn't anything to do with you and me.

80

STELLA: What do you mean? She has everything to do with us.

EVAN: No. (*He moves round L. of table.*) You say we are happy here. God! Don't I know it. I've never been so happy in my life. Because I've known there was a bond between us that was growing stronger with every hour of every day. And you've known it, too, deep in your heart, but you won't admit it.

STELLA (*impulsive*): Oh! But I do admit it . . . No. . . .

EVAN *goes towards her.*

Dear . . . dear Evan. (*Searches for words.*) You don't understand. I can feel it all in my heart, but I can't explain it. From the very first evening I was happy. Not only because of Cherry, but because of you. And all these weeks it has grown lovelier. The things you said and the things you didn't say. But even when we were not talking, when you just sat smoking a cigarette, and I sat beside you, there was something quiet about it all, and still and peaceful. Now it isn't peaceful any longer.

EVAN: Why not? What I did to you just now was a very simple thing. It's the thing that usually happens between two people when they love each other.

STELLA: But Evan . . . dear . . . don't pretend to be a child. You and I can't love each other in that way.

EVAN: You say "that way" as if I had done something repellent and unchaste. There's only one way to love, and that's to give everything, body, mind and heart. You can have all three of mine for what they're worth.

STELLA *moves away from him L.*

STELLA: You don't know what you're saying. Or if you do, I refuse to understand you. For the first time since I've known you, we're talking a different language.

81

EVAN: Are we? How?

STELLA (*very much moved; sits down on chair*): I was brought up to respect a moral code, what Cherry pleases to call my 1914 standards. I respect them still. I shall respect them all my life. Whatever I may feel in my heart, in my mind and in my body, those standards will come first. They stand like a rock in front of every feeling and every sentiment. That's where we differ—your generation and mine.

EVAN: My generation is no different from yours. Ten rather lonely, bitter years between the two. And what you say about a moral code is false. False, like every religion invented by man through fear of his own senses. You put up your rock of defence because you are afraid of what might happen if it crashed.

STELLA: I'm not afraid. Fear has nothing to do with what I feel.

EVAN: Why did you push me away, then, when I kissed you? Why did you stare at me, for one brief moment, with a queer, lost look in your eyes? That wasn't moral. That wasn't self-righteous. It was because the thing had happened that was bound to happen one day. I've loved you from the very first evening that I came into this house. God knows, I did not expect it, did not want it—but it happened. The thing is admitted, done. There's no going back on it. God forgive me if I hurt you by telling you this. I have to tell you.

STELLA: You don't hurt me. I can cope with my own feelings; they don't matter.

EVAN: What matters then?

STELLA (*with force*): Cherry matters. And the fundamental knowledge of what is right and what is wrong. The deepest thing in any man or woman. You have that

82

knowledge too. You can't escape from it. It's instinctive in every one of us.

EVAN (*kneels by her*): It isn't instinctive in me. My instinct, and my knowledge, tell me that during the past two months you've grown lovelier and younger every day, not through the help of your moral code, nor your defensive barrier, but because you've known in your heart that I was looking at you, and loving you, and you were happy about it, and glad, and gay.

STELLA (*afraid*): It isn't true.

EVAN: It is true.

STELLA: I won't have you say these things to me. (*She turns away from him.*)

EVAN: I *shall* say them to you.

There is a sound of shouting outside on the slip, confused sounds, amidst the wind and the rain.

STELLA (*distressed and unhappy*): There's someone below there on the slip. See who it is.

EVAN *goes to hook-door above slip, and opens it. He is nearly blown back by force of the wind.*

EVAN (*leaning out*): Hullo, there! What do you want?

Someone answers in a hoarse shout. We cannot hear the drift of words.

All right. I'll see to it. (*Turns back into room, refastening door.*) It's the dinghy. The tide's carried it off the slip, and it's adrift. I'll have to get hold of it.

STELLA: How? What are you going to do?

EVAN: Swim for it. It's only about ten feet away. (*Throws off his shoes, begins to roll up his trousers.*)

83

STELLA (*coming forward*): You're not to do anything of the sort. You must be mad. Let the boat sink. What does it matter?

EVAN: It won't take five seconds.

STELLA: Evan. . . . No. . . . No. I won't let you go. It's dangerous. (*She takes his arm and tries to hold him.*)

EVAN: What of it? Why should you care? Get some dry clothes for me, and a towel, and pour me out the dregs of the Nuits St. Georges.

He opens the door, which flies back against wall, and climbs down ladder into darkness. The wind tears into the room, blowing STELLA's *hair and dress as she stands there.*

STELLA (*very frightened*): Evan . . . Evan . . . Come back. (*Waits a moment, as she hears the splash into the water. She leans through the door nearly blown backwards.*) Evan? Evan? Oh. . . . (*She is half-crying by now, completely shaken and unnerved. Moves in a daze about the room, looking for dry clothes. Fetches a towel from behind the screen, and warms it before the fire. The wind has blown the candles, only the lamp burns, and perhaps a single candle, and the fire. Then she goes back again to the open door.*) Evan. . . . Evan. . . .

This time an answering shout is near, and in a moment EVAN *comes up the ladder and into the room. He shuts the door. He stands for a moment, dripping wet, smiling at her.*

Oh, thank God. . . . Here—take this.

She gives him the towel, throws the clothes on the chair, and this time, really crying, she goes over to chair by fire and sits down, her back turned to him, fumbling with her handkerchief. EVAN *tears off his wet shirt over his head and rubs himself with the towel. Then he goes*

L. to landing and changes into dry clothes, shouting to her through the door.

EVAN: The blasted painter had got jammed under the ladder. I only had to swim about a couple of yards, hanging on to the boat all the time. A very simple manœuvre, and an enjoyable one, granted a clear moonlight night. How the devil the painter jammed I don't know. Thank the Lord it did, or the dinghy would be halfway across the harbour by now. The sailing-boat is riding it out all right. I could just make out the dark shape of her in the distance. Wouldn't care to have swum out to her much. There's a dickens of a sea coming up the harbour. Funny thing, it wasn't cold at all. Rather pleasant. Perhaps it always is when it blows as hard as this.

He comes back into the room. Looks at STELLA, *who hasn't moved, but sits with her back turned, crying silently, staring at the fire.*

EVAN: What would you have done if I hadn't come back? Gone running up the village calling for help? Or got on the telephone and summoned the Lifeboat? Perhaps the Lifeboat doesn't put out for solitary drowning men. Only for ships' crews. Solitary drowning men don't matter. They must get themselves out of their own mess.

STELLA *still doesn't answer. He goes over to her, stands beside her.*

This is the second time to-day I've made you cry.

STELLA (*turning to him, crying*): You frightened me so. I know how the tide runs there beneath the slip. A hundred years ago a man was drowned there doing just that same thing.

EVAN (*very gently, but half-laughing*): A hundred years ago. All that while? (*He touches her hair.*)

85

STELLA: They talk about it in the village still. His name was Albert Pearn.

He laughs and holds her close. But she is anxious still. She feels his hands, and tries to warm them.

You're sure you're all right? You haven't caught cold?

EVAN: I'm all right. But look—this sweater is torn worse than the shirt. You'll have to find that needle and thread again.

He kneels beside her and puts his arms round her.

STELLA (*holding him close*): When you went out of that door . . . I thought you were never coming back again. Oh, not just the wind and the rain and the tide. I thought, for one terrible moment, that you wouldn't come back because of all the things I had said to you.

EVAN: I wanted you to think that.

STELLA: It was cruel of you.

EVAN: I told you I'm not the sort of person that goes round making other people happy.

STELLA: You've always made me happy, until now, until to-night.

EVAN: This was to have been our very special evening, wasn't it? The omelette *à la Esperanza,* and the Nuits St. Georges. Instead, I make you cry. Will you forgive me?

STELLA: I forgive you for everything but the last—going down on to the slip after the boat. I should have gone down into the water after you if you had not come back.

EVAN: Can you swim?

STELLA: No.

EVAN (*stands and looks down at her*): That rock of defence. It's washed away with the tide, hasn't it? (*Touches her hair.*) Don't ever build it up again. Let it stay dead for a hundred years, like Albert Pearn.

He reaches for her hands and kisses them.

STELLA: Never, never do it again.

EVAN (*gently*): Do what, my darling?

STELLA: Dive into the harbour.

EVAN (*smiles and looks at her*): Now would be the moment to paint you. Now, while you look like this. One tear still hovering in your left eye.

He touches the tear. The telephone begins ringing suddenly in the hall. There is a pause. They turn to listen.

All right. I'll go.

He goes down through doorway to room below. We can hear him answer the telephone. STELLA *moves to fireplace and lights the candles again with a taper.* EVAN *returns to the room. Stands against the door.*

STELLA: Well?

EVAN (*slowly*): It was Pam Tremayne. Cherry's going to stay with her. She can't get back because of the gale. The Ferry isn't running any more to-night.

The rain patters loudly on the skylight, and a gust of wind tears at the hooked door, but does not open it. EVAN *goes on standing at the door, his back against it, looking at* STELLA *as the curtain falls.*

CURTAIN

ACT 3

SCENE ONE

The living-room, the next morning. The hatch-door to the slip is wide open, and the sun streams through the windows. Gulls are crying. There is the early, fresh feeling of morning that comes in the west country after storm.

At rise. MRS. TUCKET *is on hands and knees before the open hatch-door, scrubbing the stone flags. After a moment she rises, takes pail to slipway, and empties it into harbour. Returns wringing out her cloth.* CHERRY *enters L.*

CHERRY: Good morning, Mrs. Tucket.

MRS. T. (*surprised*): Why, Miss Cherry! You're down bright and early. Did the sunshine bring you out of bed?

CHERRY: Haven't been to bed. At least, not in this house. I was weather-bound last night, after going to the pictures, and had to spend the night with Miss Tremayne.

MRS. T.: My dear life! Well, it *did* blow and no mistake. I've never known such a night in years. You'd think my roof was coming in. And the tide so high it was washing right in under the doorway of my place.

CHERRY (*looking from hatch*): The dinghy seems all right. Mr. Davies must have pulled her to the top of the slip. Got a cup of tea going, Mrs. Tucket?

MRS. T.: I'll get you one at once, Miss Cherry. I haven't been in to your mother yet.

CHERRY: I don't want anything to eat. Only a cup of tea. (*Looks at dish on piano, and takes an apple.*) Evan? (*Calls up steps to studio*) Evan?

MRS. TUCKET *exits L.* EVAN *appears on landing above studio steps. Stands looking down at* CHERRY.

EVAN: Hello. . . . When did you get back?

CHERRY: Just a moment ago. Lovely evening, wasn't it? Were you nearly blown to bits up there?

EVAN *doesn't answer. Comes down from studio.*

We had rather fun. We went to all the pubs within a radius of five miles after seeing the flick, and then came back and cooked kippers over the kitchen fire, and drank quantities of beer. I've had indigestion ever since. . . . Well, what do you make of our west country weather? Temperamental isn't it?

EVAN (*sits on window-sill*): Very. Your dinghy went adrift. I had to go and rescue it.

CHERRY: How?

EVAN: Took a header off the slip and swam for it.

CHERRY: What a crazy thing to do! I wish I'd seen you. With a bit of embellishment, we would get the story into the local paper. Striking headlines: "Famous Artist swept away by Tide." More grist to the gossip mill. You'd even have the reporters on the doorstep.

EVAN: I'm afraid they'd be disappointed. The dinghy was firmly attached to the sea-wall. I only found that out *after* I had taken the plunge.

Comes down C. and sits by piano.

CHERRY: Oh! That rather spoils the story. I was picturing you halfway down the harbour, with Mother screaming from the window like Bluebeard's wife. You were lucky you didn't have to swim far. If you really had got into the tideway, you wouldn't be alive to tell the tale.

MRS. TUCKET *enters with tray.*

MRS. T.: Here you are, Miss Cherry. Sure you wouldn't like a cup, too, Mr. Davies?

EVAN (*from hatch*): No, thank you, Mrs. Tucket.

MRS. T.: I went in to your mother, Miss Cherry, and she said she hadn't any time for breakfast this morning, she had far too much to do. She had all the things out of the linen cupboard and was marking them afresh, even the winter blankets.

CHERRY (*drinks tea by fireplace*): Mother gets fevers like that from time to time, and always chooses the most maddening moments. I remember she used to turn out the linen cupboard the day before Jimmy went back to school—just when he needed all her attention. We'll have to put a stop to it, or she'll have the whole house upside down. Anyway, it's going to be a lovely day. Look—the glass is rising.

MRS. T. (*finishing her dusting*): A sudden rise or a sudden fall is bad. So Joe down at the Ferry was telling me.

CHERRY: I suppose Joe held your hand all night. Nothing else for him to do once the Ferry stopped running.

MRS. T. (*pleased*): Get along, Miss Cherry. Have some respect for my grey hairs.

CHERRY: Why should I? Joe hasn't.

MRS. T.: Mr. Davies looks quite shocked.

CHERRY: Not him! He's past shocking. Aren't you, Evan? He'd hold your hand himself for twopence.

MRS. T.: Then I'll know where to come to next time! Don't forget, Mr. Davies. There's many a good tune played on an old fiddle.

MRS. TUCKET *exits L., pleased with her sally.*

CHERRY (*laughs and looks at* EVAN): Don't look so stuffy. What's the matter?

EVAN: Nothing's the matter. I merely find the thought of slap-and-tickle with Mrs. Tucket strangely repellent.

CHERRY (*looking from hatch*): Who would believe such an awful night would produce such a God-given morning? We ought to all go for a picnic or something. (*Stands outside.*) Nothing much wrong with the dinghy. Full of rainwater, that's all.

STELLA *enters, overall, perhaps, over dress.*

STELLA: Where's Cherry? Is she all right?

EVAN (*stands up*): Perfectly. Is there any reason why she shouldn't be?

STELLA (*sits at her desk*): No. . . . None at all. Aren't you painting this morning?

EVAN: No.

CHERRY enters from hatch.

CHERRY (*to* STELLA): Hullo, darling. You look awfully domestic.

STELLA: Well, how was it? Did you enjoy your film?

CHERRY: Wonderful. But it wasn't Ingrid Bergman after all. It was an old re-hash of Grace Moore's "One Night of Love." What are you going to do, darling? Start on the store cupboard when you've finished the linen?

STELLA: Very probably. I've got some telephoning to do first.

CHERRY: You can't telephone; there're about fifty telephone lines down between here and Plymouth. If you want any fish, there isn't any. I saw Phillips as I came through the town. And the post's late. So as far as the outside world is concerned, you've had it. (*Looks impishly from* STELLA *to* EVAN.)

STELLA turns away.

(*Pause.*) Well, I suppose I ought to go and bale out the dinghy.

EVAN (*looks at* STELLA): I'll do it for you.

CHERRY: How very noble of you. Becoming boat-minded all of a sudden? I'll give you a hand down the slip.

She exits from hatch. EVAN *pauses a moment, then follows* CHERRY *out of hatch-door.* STELLA *stands quite still. She hears* CHERRY *laugh. She looks unhappy, haunted. She is trying to make up her mind about something. Tries the telephone, but there is no answer.*

STELLA (*calling through to hall*): Mrs. Tucket . . .

MRS. T. (*standing in doorway*): Did you call me, m'm?

STELLA: Yes. . . . The telephone isn't working; the lines are down, or something's wrong, and I must see Mr. Hanson this morning . . . it's very important. Do you think you could go up the hill and ask him to call in, as soon as he can?

MRS. T. (*wiping hands on apron*): Why, of course, m'm. I'll go at once. It won't take a minute.

STELLA: Thank you. (*Goes back to desk, nervy.*)

CHERRY (*laughing, coming in through hatch*): I don't know what's come over Evan.

STELLA: Why?

CHERRY: Insisted on doing the boat himself, and told me to come in and look after you. Really very filial. I'm quite touched. What's the matter, darling? You look awfully preoccupied.

STELLA *gets up from her desk.*

STELLA: Nothing's the matter. I must go and tidy. Robert is coming in directly.

CHERRY: Robert keeps himself very aloof these days. I think Pam must be right.

STELLA: Right about what?

CHERRY: According to her, and to various other people, Robert doesn't come here any more because he dislikes Evan.

STELLA (*nervy*): That's absurd!

93

CHERRY (*sits on sofa*): I quite agree. And even if it's true, I couldn't care less. Robert is your property, not mine.

STELLA (*makes a decision with a great effort*): Darling . . . I've got to talk to you . . . very seriously.

CHERRY (*blankly*): What about?

STELLA: About—about you and Evan. It's not right for us all to live here together. You ought to be alone, the two of you.

CHERRY: Don't be so ridiculous.

STELLA: I'm not ridiculous. I know I'm right. I've known it for some time. (*She moves restlessly across the room.*)

CHERRY (*aghast*): But we love being here, and being with you. Evan is a different person from what he used to be in London. He's happy and well, and scarcely touches whisky. And he's doing good work, what's more. You don't know how good.

STELLA (*sits down on chair below piano*): Yes, I do, dear. But it would be better work, and happier for you both, if you had the place to yourselves. I'm talking plain common sense. Three is a hopeless number, and always has been. Living with relations is all very well for a time, but eventually a man needs to feel that he is living in his own home—that he isn't just a guest in someone else's house. I know how Evan loves this place and you —but you'd love it so much more if it belonged to you— if you lived here on your own.

CHERRY: I just don't understand. Why bring this up suddenly, out of the blue? (*Gets up—goes towards her mother, bewildered.*) What has Evan been saying to you? You both looked queer just now. If he has been rude or unkind to you, I shall never forgive him.

STELLA (*distressed*): He hasn't been rude to me . . . or unkind. All this has been at the back of my mind for many weeks. Somehow the storm last night brought it very close. I lay awake, and thought about you both; but at the same time I thought about myself. If it's not right for you and Evan to live here with me, neither is it right for me to live here with you. Cherry—what would you say if I told you I had made up my mind to marry Robert?

CHERRY (*stares at* STELLA *in horror*): Oh! Mother!

STELLA: Why not? Yes, I know, we've joked about it always, haven't we? You and Jimmy and I—the "routes" proposal. We've made a mockery of it; we've been unjust and unfair.

CHERRY (*angry, reproachful*): You've never talked like this before. The times you've laughed about Robert, and that dreary, awful house of his, full of ships' models and stuffed birds! You'd go mad with horror if you lived there.

STELLA: The house itself is charming, and so is the garden. Only neglected, that's all. And, anyway, he's my age, my generation, we understand each other.

She rises and moves R.

CHERRY (*challenging*): Are you going to tell him all this when he comes this morning?

STELLA (*defiant*): Probably. Why?

CHERRY (*very upset*): All right, then. Go ahead. If you want to make a crashing mistake, do so. It's not for your daughter to stop you. (*She turns away.*)

STELLA (*appealing*): Cherry . . .

CHERRY (*bitter, not turning round*): What?

STELLA (*she might have said so much, but she cannot. She gestures with her hand*): Nothing. . . . Nothing. . . .

She exits L., very moved.

CHERRY (*nearly in tears, goes to hatch and calls out*): Evan? Come here. I want you.

CHERRY goes back and stands by fireplace. EVAN comes in through hatch-door, wringing out an old cloth.

EVAN: What's the matter?

CHERRY: What's wrong with Mother?

EVAN: What do you mean? (*Throws cloth on to slip.*)

CHERRY: You didn't throw one of your moods at her last night, did you? Sulk, or get drunk, or something?

EVAN: I did not.

CHERRY (*tearful*): What's happened to her, then? She's been talking a lot of absolute tripe about clearing out of here and leaving the house to us. Says we ought to have the place to ourselves. And, anyway, that she's not happy living here any more, and that she wants to marry Robert.

EVAN (*very softly*): God! (*Stands staring at CHERRY.*)

CHERRY: She was perfectly all right yesterday. Has she gone crackers, or what? Oh, darling, if she goes and flings herself at his head through some mistaken idea of helping us, I don't know what I should do. I simply adore her. (*She is nearly crying. Turns her back on EVAN.*)

EVAN (*slowly*): Do you?

CHERRY: She's the only person in life who matters, except you. I know I tease her and tell her she has a pre-1914 mentality, but she knows very well that's the chief reason I love her. She's only got to ask me to cut my throat, and I'd do it on the spot.

EVAN (*moved*): You never talked like this before. Never to me. I thought you took Stella for granted. You show your affection in an odd way, you know.

CHERRY (*in a muffled voice*): I'm not very good at telling people when I love them. That's always been my trouble.

EVAN (*quietly*): Has it? (*He stares at her a moment, then goes R. and pours some whisky into a glass. There is a pause.*)

CHERRY: Bit early for that, isn't it?

EVAN: Much too early.

CHERRY: I'd have some myself if it didn't make me sick. I feel lousy, anyhow. (*Looks in mirror.*) My face wants washing.

EVAN (*gently, half teasing*): It always does.

CHERRY (*smiles at him wistfully*): That's one of the nice, solid things about our marriage, anyhow. No false sentiment. We know exactly where we are with each other. We might have been married for years. Oh, Evan . . . what are we going to *do?* (*Moves up to him impulsively.*)

EVAN (*slowly*): I don't know. . . .

Sound of voice in hall, and MRS. TUCKET *speaking.*

MRS. T. (*off*): Will you go in, sir? I think Mrs. Martyn is there.

CHERRY (*agitated, going towards hatch*): Oh! . . . There *is* Robert! I can't face him, I shall only say something terribly tactless and make things twenty times worse. You'll *have* to cope with him.

She runs off through hatch-door. EVAN *listens, pours out more whisky. Stands thinking.* ROBERT *enters L.*

ROBERT: Hullo, hullo! Good morning.

EVAN: Good morning.

ROBERT: Filthy night, wasn't it?

EVAN: Stinking.

ROBERT: Did the rain come in the attic roof?

EVAN: If it did, I didn't notice it.

ROBERT: Oh. Well, it used to at one time, when I used the attic as a sail-loft.

EVAN: I didn't know the attic was ever a haunt of yours.

ROBERT: Didn't you? You forget, I've known the family for over fifteen years.

EVAN: Oh, no, I don't. I remember it only too well. It gives you a great advantage over everybody else. Have some of this? (*Holds up whisky.*)

ROBERT (*turns away*): No, thank you. I had breakfast barely an hour ago.

EVAN: What of it. So did I. (*Pours more whisky into glass.*) I sometimes think, you know, that you and I are very much alike.

ROBERT: I can't say the thought has ever struck me. I can't think of two people less alike.

EVAN: On the surface—no. But inside, and when it comes to fundamentals—yes. We both have a tenacity of purpose that never weakens. We both have emotions that we are able to keep well under control only by the force of iron determination, and where our affections are concerned, once our choice has been made, we remain constant to the end of time.

ROBERT: A very pretty speech. But what exactly it refers to, and why at this hour of the morning, I haven't the slightest idea.

EVAN: No? . . . Forget it, then. It doesn't really matter, one way or the other. But what you said about the attic made me think. One hour in the balance, against fifteen years. There's a hell of a lot of leeway to make up. You win, every time, on paper. You know, another glass of whisky and I shall become quite eloquent. What a fool I've been these past weeks, living on fruit and lemonade. Quite fatal to genius. In time it would have ruined me. Whisky is, and always will be, the one and only drink for someone of my temperament, at ten in the morning.

He climbs unsteadily upstairs to studio.

ROBERT: I'm glad to say I never touch it before six in the evening.

EVAN: That's where you make your one mistake in life. It settles the stomach, steadies the nerves, and makes you say damn-all to the woman you love.

As he speaks, STELLA *enters L. She has taken off her overall, and carries a plate of fruit in one hand; also lemonade.*

(*Leaning over rail, below studio.*) Ah! How extremely appropriate! The lady of the house in question, bearing in her hands, Robert, a bunch of grapes. For you, of course. Sweet, I trust, not sour. Some whisky, Stella?

It is obvious both to STELLA *and to* ROBERT *that he is more than slightly drunk.* STELLA *stares at the whisky, and then at* EVAN.

ROBERT: I believe you wanted to see me about something, Stella. Perhaps it would be more convenient if I called some other time. (*He speaks to* STELLA, *ignoring* EVAN.)

EVAN: Much more convenient. We're all very busy at the moment turning out the linen cupboard.

ROBERT (*to* STELLA): If it's impossible for you to have any privacy here, come up to my house. That is, if the business is urgent.

STELLA: It is—rather urgent.

EVAN (*still leaning over stair-rail*): Oh, come. It can't be as urgent as all that. After all, you've waited ten years or more without coming to a decision. Surely an hour or so one way or the other wouldn't kill you?

ROBERT: Is Cherry home? Because if she is, it mightn't be a bad idea if she persuaded this fellow to lie down. He appears to be suffering from a hang-over.

EVAN: Not a hang-over, old boy. Merely the beginning of a brand-new bout. I'm still in very good form. I shan't start knocking anyone's head off for another twenty-four hours at least.

100

STELLA (*slowly*): I think you had better go, Bob. I know how to deal with Evan.

ROBERT (*contemptuous*): The Services taught me a method that would be very effective with you, young man.

EVAN: Did they? I never discovered it. What do they use? Hypnosis, or Yogi, or a dash of both? You see, Robert, I genuinely want to be cured. I've tried everything. Lemon and glucose . . . eating raw liver . . . breathing deeply in front of an open window. . . . Nothing works.

ROBERT (*turning away*): I shall be at home all day if you want me, Stella. You and Cherry had better come up to lunch. And if you've got any more of that stuff in the house, you'd be wise to put it away under lock and key.

ROBERT *exits L.* STELLA *comes down centre.*

STELLA (*to* EVAN): How dare you behave like this in my house?

EVAN (*comes swiftly downstairs*): I'm sorry. I had to get rid of him. There wasn't any other way.

STELLA (*stares at him, bewildered*): You're not . . . drunk after all.

EVAN: It takes rather more than a few whiskies to do that. Of course I'm not drunk. The point is, the object has been achieved. You haven't spoken to Robert alone. Nor are you going to.

STELLA (*moving to fireplace, her back turned to him*): What makes you think I wanted to see Robert alone?

EVAN: Cherry told me. You were going to ask him to marry you.

101

STELLA: And why not?

EVAN: You don't love him, and you never will.

STELLA: Robert has loved me faithfully and devotedly for fifteen years. You told me I was lonely. You're right. I am lonely. By marrying Robert, I shall put an end to all future loneliness.

EVAN: It's no use. It won't work. Not that sort of lie.

STELLA: I'm not lying, I'm telling you the truth.

EVAN: There isn't one word of truth in anything you've said. Your whole body is a lie—the back of your head, your shoulders, your hands touching the mantelpiece. I know exactly what has happened to you. I knew exactly how it would be when I said good night and let you go. The rock of defence has been built up again in a virulent, hopeless form, with Robert as guardian angel. God! Why does the morning have to do this to you? Look at me!

A pause. STELLA *turns, gestures with her hand.*

STELLA: Evan . . . I can't go on living in this house with you and Cherry. Not after the things we said to each other last night.

EVAN (*goes to her—takes her hands—quietly*): The things we said last night shall be forgotten. I love you well enough for that. Kissing you shall be a thing that never ever happened. Perhaps you don't believe me.

STELLA: I do believe you. I believe you have a will of iron that I don't possess myself. You could go on being here and everything seem just the same as it was before. I can't do that. I'm not made that way. (*She moves away from him R.*)

EVAN: I don't understand.

STELLA (*fiercely*): No . . . your generation *doesn't* understand.

EVAN: Would you throw away all companionship, understanding, affection—because of the things I told you, that you didn't want to hear?

STELLA (*sits on piano stool and faces him*): But I did want to hear them. That's what I can't forgive. That's what has made me treacherous and disloyal. . . . Evan, when I looked in the glass just now, the morning light was very merciless. The true Stella stared me in the face. You should have finished your portrait then.

EVAN: Who *is* the true Stella?

STELLA: Someone selfish and hard, with strange, frightening thoughts. Someone who in a few hours has become jealous of her own daughter. (*Turns away.*)

EVAN: What are you trying to tell me?

STELLA: Everything. . . . Nothing. (*Gets up; walks to window.*) All I know is that the world has become a different place. I feel bewildered and lost and frightened in a desperate sort of way. Not a way I understand.

EVAN: Stella . . . darling. . . .

He goes towards her, but she puts up her hands.

STELLA: No. . . . (*She backs away, holding on to studio stairs.*) You see . . . we're both different people from the ones we were yesterday.

EVAN: Perhaps we are. And if you believe that, can you *still* leave this house and marry Robert?

He walks swiftly to where she stands by the stairs. She watches him. She does not move.

Can you?

At this moment there is a loud knocking at the front door, and CHERRY *can be heard speaking.*

CHERRY: All right. I'll take it.

CHERRY *comes through to living-room with telegram.*

Telegram for you, darling. The boy's waiting for an answer.

STELLA (*pulls herself together with great effort*): Telegram? Who from? What about?

CHERRY: I haven't the slightest idea, sweetheart. You'd better open it and see. (*Gives telegram. Flops down on sofa.*)

STELLA (*looks around her*): What did I do with my glasses?

EVAN (*quietly*): They're up in the studio. And you don't need them. Not in the merciless light of morning.

STELLA *looks at him. Then goes across to open hatch to read telegram.*

CHERRY: Well? Anything exciting?

STELLA (*shaken and alarmed. Rather dazed*): It's from Jimmy. His ship arrived in Plymouth last night, and he's had some sort of accident. His leg, he says. . . . He's broken a bone. . . . He's coming home on sick leave to-day. (*Moves down to* CHERRY.)

CHERRY: How typical of Jimmy. Always turns up like a bad penny. Just when he isn't wanted.

STELLA (*anxious, loving*): He is wanted. He's always wanted.

CHERRY: The little lost lamb, returned to the fold.

EVAN (*softly*): Not the lost lamb. The homing pigeon. . . . Well, the boy's waiting, Stella. Don't you want to send a message back?

STELLA: Yes. . . . Yes, of course. Have you a pencil?

She sits by CHERRY.

EVAN: I'll write it for you. What do you want me to say?

He sees she can't concentrate, takes pencil from pocket and an old envelope, and waits for her.

STELLA (*after pause, slowly*): Put: "Your room ready for you as always, my darling. Dear love." And sign it "Mother."

EVAN *is busy writing as*

THE CURTAIN FALLS

SCENE TWO

Six hours later. The sun is low in the west, and comes through hatch door to carpet.
JIMMY *is lying on the sofa, his leg propped up on a cushion. He is throwing darts, unsuccessfully, at dartboard by mantelpiece.* CHERRY *is lying on the floor, reading a book. A noisy gramophone is playing a strident Rumba.* EVAN *sits by the open hatch, looking out on to the harbour. We must feel that he listens to the children's conversation, but is not of the party.*

JIMMY: It's not a question of looks at all. It's the way they move, the way they smile, the way they set out to entertain a fellow. I tell you, our women just don't begin to compare with the women of South America.

CHERRY (*not looking up from book*): Join the Navy and see the world.

JIMMY: It's no joking matter. I'm serious. The whole feminine outlook to life is different, once you get across the Atlantic. You don't seem to realise what happens, Cherry, when chaps like us go ashore at some of these places.

CHERRY: Yes, I do. You call it showing the flag—and it costs the British taxpayer millions.

She dodges dart thrown by JIMMY.

And they can't even teach you to aim straight.

JIMMY: You're jealous because you've never been out of England. That reminds me. . . . Did I tell you the story about the girl, the Scotsman and the submarine?

CHERRY: You did. And I *don't* want to hear it again.

JIMMY: Oh! . . . Well, there's an even funnier one about an old woman, a bottle of brandy, and a cockatoo.

CHERRY: Shut up. Mother might hear you.

JIMMY (*moving restlessly*): Blast this infernal foot! I say, Cherry, I feel like a glass of beer.

CHERRY: Well, shout for one, then.

JIMMY (*shouts*): Mother! (*To himself*) Lot of fun this is going to be, lying around like a cripple for God knows how long. *Mother!*

STELLA (*from hall*): Coming, darling.

She enters with a heavy basket of logs, which she puts down by the fire, panting a little. EVAN, *turning his head, sees this, and stands up, but is too late to help her.*

JIMMY: Get me some beer, will you? And another packet of cigarettes. Where have you been for the last hour?

STELLA: Seeing to a hundred and one things, darling. Mrs. Tucket goes home midday Saturdays. I'll get your beer.

CHERRY: Bring two tankards, Mummy. I'll have some, too.

STELLA goes to cupboard to take out tankards and beer, but EVAN has forestalled her, and is there first. He puts the tankards and the beer on the tray for her, saying nothing. She looks at him a moment, then turns away. EVAN sits on one of the steps to studio. Gramophone makes deafening sound.

STELLA: Oh, Jimmy! No. . . . No. . . . Turn it off. (*She has her hands to her ears.*) It is making such a racket.

JIMMY (*surprised*): Sorry. I didn't notice it. (*Turns it off.*) Damn good tune, I think.

STELLA: I'll hear it later. (*Gives* JIMMY *and* CHERRY *their beer.*)

JIMMY: Why don't you have some? Do you good.

STELLA: I don't want any, darling.

JIMMY: Afraid of putting on weight round the midriff?

STELLA: That wouldn't worry me. How's your foot?

JIMMY (*irritable*): Giving me infernal gyp. Can't you loosen the bandage, or something?

STELLA: The doctor will be here directly. He'll do it for you properly. (*Bends to look at foot.*)

JIMMY: Oh no, he won't. He'll make it a hundred times worse. The blighters always do. Ow! Look out!

STELLA: Sorry, sweetie . . . I can't see the knot.

JIMMY: Got your glasses?

STELLA: No.

She looks about her. She turns, moves to look for them. EVAN, saying nothing, takes the glasses from his pocket, and gives them to her. We must feel that this moment is somehow significant for both of them.

(*Almost unheard*) Thank you.

She goes and kneels by sofa, loosens bandage. EVAN, leaning on rail of steps, watches her.

JIMMY: To think I had every chance of being chosen for scrum-half this season, and this had to happen.

CHERRY: If you will practise rugger in a gun-turret, and then slip up on your backside, what else can you expect but a broken foot?

JIMMY: It wasn't in a gun-turret, you great ass. I was in the gun-*room*. And if that greasy little fool McFadden hadn't pushed the piano on top of me, the thing would never have happened.

CHERRY: Item. One midshipman's foot. One midshipman's face. One broken piano. No wonder the Naval Estimates are always high.

JIMMY: Oh, go and boil yourself.

They have been at this sort of thing for years.

STELLA: Children. . . . Children. (*She rises and pats the cushion behind* JIMMY's *head. Bends and kisses him.*) Is that better, darling?

JIMMY (*smiling up at her*): Much better. (*He pats her on the face.*)

EVAN, *leaning on rail, turns and moves up stairs to studio.*

(*To* STELLA) Come on, sit down a minute, darling, can't you? I've hardly had a word with you all day.

STELLA (*sitting by him on sofa*): That's not fair. I was playing backgammon with you for two hours after lunch.

JIMMY: Yes, and damn absent-minded you were, too. Didn't know what you were doing half the time.

STELLA: I forget how to play when you're away so much.

JIMMY: Get Evan to give you a game then when I'm not here. He's terrific. Beat me hollow before tea. Didn't you, Evan? Hullo—where is Evan?

They all look up towards studio.

CHERRY: Gone to brood over his pictures, I expect.

JIMMY: Don't you brood with him?

CHERRY: Not I. You don't know my husband. He's the cat that walks by himself.

JIMMY: Well, I must say, you haven't picked too badly, old girl. What do you think of your son-in-law, Mother?

STELLA: I'm very fond of him.

109

JIMMY: Come to think of it, he's nearer your generation than he is ours.

CHERRY: You ought to see Evan and Mother in the evenings. Positively World War One. Evan sits at the piano and plays waltzes, and Mother gazes at the fire looking sentimental. Almost breaks your heart.

JIMMY: How absolutely wizard. Will you put up a show for us to-night, Mother? I feel like a damn good cry.

STELLA *gets up from sofa.*

Oh, hell—now I've set her on the move again, just as we were getting cosy. How's the boy-friend, darling?

STELLA (*sensitive*): What do you mean?

JIMMY: Come off it. Don't be coy. The faithful Robert, of course. Has he popped the question lately? Now's the time to consider it, with Cherry safely off your hands.

CHERRY *makes warning faces at* JIMMY, *who looks puzzled.*

Eh? Oh . . . (*Begins to whistle.*) I say, I'm uncommonly thirsty. Can you produce another pint of beer?

STELLA: I think so. (*Goes to cupboard.*) Will you see the doctor here, or in your room?

JIMMY: In my room. The light's better there, and he can peel off the bandages and have a proper squint.

STELLA: In that case, I'll go and get clean towels, and see that the water is hot. (*She is restless—must be occupied.*)

JIMMY: No hurry.

110

STELLA: I'd rather do it now. Get it done with. (*Pauses a moment by stairs, glancing up to studio. Hesitates, then exits L. to hall.*)

JIMMY: What's up? Why the warning face?

CHERRY: I was going to tell you, but there hasn't been a chance. Robert's a tricky subject at the moment. There's a hell of a drama going on.

JIMMY: What's happened? Have they fallen out?

CHERRY: I wish to heaven they had. . . . She says she's going to marry him.

JIMMY: My God! No! What, suddenly? Without any reason?

CHERRY: No reason at all. Except she harped on the fact that Evan and I ought to be alone. That it was bad for us to all be here together.

JIMMY: What utter rot. . . . I say, they do get on, don't they?

CHERRY: Who? Evan and Mother? Oh, yes. Terrific buddies. That's why being here has been so perfect. Everything dead easy. Of course, he *is* a newcomer to the family. We have to remember that. He doesn't understand Mother like we do.

JIMMY: No; of course not.

CHERRY (*moving about room*): Men are so damn selfish. What if Robert has been pitching her some yarn about being lonely, and that he can't live without her—she's so incredibly soft-hearted she'd fall for it at once. If she thought she was making anyone unhappy, she just couldn't take it. She'd feel she'd committed a crime.

111

JIMMY: That's the trouble with her generation. They always will take everything so damn seriously.

CHERRY: I know. *Fatal*. Why can't they behave like us? (*Stands by fireplace.*)

JIMMY: I suppose seeing you and Evan together all the time hasn't made her feel out of things? Sounds rather silly, but you know what I mean.

CHERRY (*shakes her head*): Doesn't work out. Evan and I are so matter-of-fact.

JIMMY: Great relief, I should think.

CHERRY (*uncertain*): Yes. . . .

JIMMY: It's awfully embarrassing as a rule staying in a house where two people have just got married, or become engaged, or something. They keep looking at each other all the time, and having private jokes, until you don't know where to put yourself. If you and Evan had been like that, I could understand Mother getting fed up.

CHERRY: Yes, you would. But Mother's different. The closer people are, the happier she becomes.

JIMMY: Well, it's no use being morbid about it. If she begins talking to me about Robert, I shall just rag her frightfully and see what effect that has. There's a saying, isn't there, that ridicule kills anything?

CHERRY: I don't believe she'd take ragging at the moment. She has that look behind her eyes that means the slightest thing would make her cry.

JIMMY: Oh, well, the only thing to do is to keep her very busy, and very cheerful. Round games every evening, and lots to do all day. Shrieks of fun and roars of laughter from morning till night. You leave it to me.

CHERRY: It won't work.

JIMMY: It's got to work. We can't have her walking off and marrying Robert. What the hell would happen to me?

He puts on another noisy record.

CHERRY: Selfish little brute. The whole point is what the hell would happen to Mother.

EVAN *comes on to top of stairs and leans over. He has to shout, because of gramophone.*

EVAN: Cherry?

CHERRY: Hullo.

EVAN: Is that telephone working again yet?

CHERRY: I don't know. I'll try it and see. (*Gets up from floor, and goes to telephone. Jerks receiver up and down.*) Dead as mutton. Not a flicker of life. . . . Oh, hang on. Wait a second. . . . Exchange . . . are you there? Can you hear me? . . . No; you're very faint. . . . Right, thank you. (*Replaces receiver.*) They say the men are still working on the line. They'll give us a ring when it's O.K. It won't be long now.

EVAN: Thank you. (*Comes down the stairs from studio.*)

CHERRY: Do you want me to get through to someone for you?

EVAN: No. Don't bother. It doesn't matter. . . . (*Comes down room towards sofa.*)

JIMMY: Cherry, old girl, if you're up, you might go and tell Mother I would fancy spaghetti and cheese for supper after all, with some of that tomato sauce. She knows the kind I mean.

CHERRY: Greedy little beast. Anything else?

JIMMY: Yes. Tell her to open that bottle of burgundy. There was one left last time I was on leave.

CHERRY: Saw it on the dust-heap this morning. You've had it?

Exits L. JIMMY switches off gramophone.

EVAN: How's the foot?

JIMMY: Lousy. And it will be worse directly when the medico has a go at it.

EVAN: Fill yourself up with whisky first; then you won't feel it.

JIMMY: Don't you worry. I've got some rum upstairs, full strength. Straight from Jamaica. Like some?

EVAN (*smiling*): Don't think so. Not at the moment.

JIMMY: What have you been doing up there? (*Nods at studio.*)

EVAN: Going through some pictures. Choosing the ones for export, and throwing out the rest.

JIMMY: Sounds very business-like and commercial. What do you do with duds?

EVAN: Send 'em to the R.A.

JIMMY: Will you paint my portrait one day?

EVAN: Perhaps I will. But not till you're First Sea Lord. It wouldn't pay me! (*Lights cigarette and sits on arm of sofa.*)

JIMMY: It must be queer to be an artist. I suppose you see things in people's faces that chaps like me can't see at all.

EVAN: Yes . . . sometimes.

JIMMY: All kinds of hidden thoughts and feelings. Ugh! It's a bit creepy when you come to think of it.

EVAN: Perhaps it is.

JIMMY: I remember once when I was a kid I did a drawing of a ship I thought was jolly good. And then my father asked to look at it, and I felt ashamed, in a funny sort of way, and I went out and chucked it on a bonfire in the garden.

EVAN: Very wise of you. I've never thought of that.

JIMMY: We might have a bonfire with your throw-outs, in this room.

EVAN: We might. (*Looks down at* JIMMY *with an expression on his face, half odd, half amused.*) Would you enjoy it?

JIMMY: It would make a good old blaze.

EVAN *rises, goes up studio steps, and returns with a canvas, which he has stripped from its frame.*

EVAN: This isn't exactly a throw-out. It's too personal for export, and too damn good for the R.A.

He stands looking at canvas, before the fire, while JIMMY *tries to look, but cannot.*

115

JIMMY: Let's have a squint at it. Oh, you rotter. You might show me.

STELLA *comes into the room L.*

It's a woman, isn't it?

EVAN: It is. (*Looks over sofa at* STELLA.)

JIMMY: Naked and unashamed?

EVAN: No. Clothed, and in her right mind.

JIMMY: Were you in love with her?

EVAN: I shall love her all my life.

JIMMY: Good for you. I don't know what you see in her myself. Good old Cherry!

EVAN: Cherry? Oh, yes. . . . Well, here goes. . . . There she burns. (*Tears canvas in two pieces, and throws on to fire.*)

STELLA (*coming forward, impulsive*): No. . . . No. . . . (*Kneels by fire, but sees it is hopeless. Sinks back on heels, looks up at* EVAN.) Why?

She is very distressed. EVAN *does not answer.*

JIMMY: He's bats. Completely bats. It might have made a hell of a lot of dough.

EVAN: I wouldn't want it to.

The canvas burns.

JIMMY: There she goes. A masterpiece lost to the world. What could have been. What still could be, perhaps, if Mother had liked to burn her hands to blazes.

EVAN: Too late for that.

The ship's bell rings by front door.

STELLA: There's the doctor.

JIMMY: Give us a hand up, chaps.

They help him to rise.

I warn you both. If he hurts me, I'll scream the place down.

EVAN *hands him his stick.*

I hope he's careful. I'm one of those little boys that can't stand pain.

He hobbles off L. with STELLA. EVAN *stands looking down at fire.* STELLA *comes back silently and stands beside him. The light gradually fades from outside.*

STELLA: *Why* did you burn it?

EVAN: You know why.

STELLA: You could have given it to me.

EVAN: No. The day might come when you would have shared it with someone else. With Robert, if you're going to marry him.

STELLA: That won't ever happen.

EVAN: Are you sure?

STELLA: Quite sure.

EVAN: What decided you?

STELLA: Does it matter?

117

EVAN: It does—to me.

Pause. STELLA *sits on sofa.*

STELLA (*slowly*): You remember, when I was doing Jimmy's bandage, I couldn't find my glasses. I looked around, and I realised that I hadn't used them all the day, that the last time I had worn them was in the studio last night. I remembered how you knelt beside me. . . . And then, as I got up just now, and you gave me back my glasses without a word—there was something in the way you looked at me—I knew I could never marry Robert, or anyone else. . . . Simple, wasn't it?

EVAN: Very simple. It's rather strange that you should feel that.

STELLA: Why?

EVAN: Because when I gave you back those glasses I was making up my mind about the future, too.

STELLA: Whose future?

EVAN: Cherry's—and yours—and mine.

STELLA: What are you going to do?

EVAN: The only thing I can do. Go away from here.

The telephone gives a faint tinkle.

No; you don't have to answer that. It means the line is working again, after the gale.

STELLA: When you say—go away from here—do you mean go away to live—taking Cherry with you?

EVAN: Isn't *that* what you want me to do?

118

STELLA (*very moved*): Yes. . . . And you'll look after Cherry—you'll make her happy?

EVAN: I'll try. . . . Queer, isn't it? But you are the only one who matters—to both of us. I don't know who loves you most. Cherry, or me.

He moves behind sofa.

Funny, isn't it, how one can be woken with a jolt by little trivial things. I watched you this afternoon, and when I saw you, sitting there with Jimmy, I was reminded of all sorts of things that I hadn't thought about for years. All this afternoon, I've kept remembering. Seeing you and Jimmy together has opened a door that has been shut to me, for a very long while.

STELLA (*gently*): Tell me.

EVAN: There's no more to tell. . . . It hurt at first, but I won't let it hurt any more. . . . I'd like you to be proud of me one day. I'd like to do something that will make you feel—all this has been worth while.

STELLA (*with feeling*): I *am* proud of you now. Oh, not of your painting; that will always be part of me from now on, exciting and wonderful. I'm proud of you because you have decided to do this thing which is hard and bitter for us both—without my asking. . . . (*Pause.*) It will be New York, won't it?

EVAN: I expect so.

STELLA (*seeing, as it were, in a flash, the future, softly*): It will be exciting for Cherry. A new life . . . a new world, seeing things she has never seen before. When you do decide to go from here there must be no farewells, no last moments, no waving goodbye across the Ferry?

She rises from sofa, moves to fireplace.

EVAN: I promise.

STELLA: You'll have to apologise to Robert, you know. He thinks you're heading for D.T.'s.

EVAN: He wouldn't be far wrong. I think that's exactly what I shall head for—once I'm the other side of the Atlantic.

STELLA: If you did, it would break my heart.

EVAN: Would it?

STELLA: Yes.

EVAN: I'll remember that.

STELLA (*sits down on chair by fire, her head against the cushion*): I wonder if Jimmy will want to play back-gammon all the evening.

EVAN: I'm afraid he will. Why?

STELLA: I'd like to have gone to bed early, and slept with-out a break until to-morrow morning. . . . I'm very tired.

She does not realise how deeply these words touch his heart.

EVAN (*gently*): Stella.

STELLA: Yes?

EVAN: I want to kiss you now, this minute, more than any-thing else in the world.

STELLA (*looking across at him*): Why?

EVAN: You'll know why—presently.

There is a shout in the distance from JIMMY *of* "Mother." STELLA *gestures with her hand and rises.*

All right. Go to him.

She smiles.

STELLA: Coming, dear. (*Exits L.*)

The telephone rings loudly. EVAN *stares at it, then goes and lifts receiver.*

EVAN: Is it clear now? Then I want Penzance 170. Thank you. . . . I'll hold on. . . . (*Pause.*) Is that Western Union? My name is Davies. Evan Davies. I sent a cable to New York yesterday morning. . . . That's right. . . . Good. . . . You've got the name and address. Well, I want to send another cancelling the one I sent yesterday. . . . Yes. Put "Accept your offer. Going London to-night. Will make all arrangements from there." Thank you. That's all.

Replaces receiver. Glances at his watch, and goes upstairs to studio. Returns with small suitcase, and overcoat. Puts them on floor beside hatch-door. CHERRY *enters L. from hall.*

EVAN: Fill my cigarette case, will you?

CHERRY: I thought I heard the telephone. (*Takes case; fills it.*)

EVAN: You did. I answered it. It was for me.

CHERRY: Anything important? (*Looks at suitcase.*)

EVAN: Very important. I've got to catch the night train for London. (*He kneels to fasten suitcase.*)

121

CHERRY: Oh, darling . . . Whatever for? What's happened?

Pause.

Sorry. . . .

EVAN: What about?

CHERRY: Our arrangement when we married. Never to ask each other questions.

EVAN: It takes a bit of doing sometimes. I don't make a very satisfactory husband, do I?

CHERRY: I wouldn't want you any different.

EVAN: No? I can't think of any other person who'd put up with me.

CHERRY: That's rather lucky, from my point of view.

She kneels to help him.

EVAN: I'll tell you something. I've decided to accept that offer from New York. It means loads of work, different from anything I've done before. Will you play?

CHERRY: You *know* I'll play. Oh, Evan—how wonderful.

EVAN: Not a word to anyone, you understand? This is our secret, yours and mine.

CHERRY (*nods*): H'm.

EVAN: I'll telephone you to-morrow evening from London, when I've found out more about it. There'll be heaps to do. Packing, and so on. And our passages to book. You can follow up with our things in a day or two. It will be lots of fun.

CHERRY (*happy*): It will be terribly exciting. I quite thought you had refused the offer, and didn't want to go.

EVAN: Did you? You should have known me better. (*Pats her face.*) Ours has been a funny sort of marriage up to date, hasn't it?

CHERRY: I don't think so.

EVAN: You're very loyal. (*Pats her trousers.*) You'll have to wear skirts to the ankles in New York.

CHERRY: I shan't mind. It will give me glamour.

EVAN: You've got it already, funny-face, but you don't know how to use it. Don't worry. You'll learn. Shall I fill my flask? No; I won't. (*Holds up flask to light, then puts it in pocket.*) I'll walk about with it in my pocket from now on, as a symbol of maturity. It will help to remind me that I've grown to man's estate.

CHERRY: I should hope so.

EVAN: Ah, but I hadn't, you know. That's been my trouble.

CHERRY: I've never noticed it. . . . You know, darling, it will be a hell of a wrench leaving here, for both of us, but it will be worth it. You're going to do better work in New York than you've ever done in your life before.

EVAN: What makes you think that?

CHERRY: A sort of hunch. Mother would call it—intuition. That reminds me. There isn't a dining-car on the evening train. You'll need some sandwiches. I'll go and tell her. (*She moves to door L.*)

EVAN: No, wait a minute. (*He gets up. Goes to desk. Scribbles on paper.*) Stella and I were talking about this New York offer before the cable came. I told her that one of these days I'd be out of the house and she wouldn't know I'd gone. I bet her five quid I'd get away with it, and she said it would be impossible. I'm going to write my goodbyes and stick them on the piano. She'll think it a terrific joke.

CHERRY: But—are you sure? It sounds a cruel sort of joke.

EVAN: Not at all. She'll understand. (*Continues writing.*)

CHERRY: You know, Evan . . . I've suddenly thought. If we go away, Mother will have the house to herself again, won't she, except for Jimmy?

EVAN: She will.

CHERRY: Were you thinking of her when the cable came?

EVAN: I was thinking of you both. (*Gets up, envelope in hand.*)

CHERRY: What did you say to her?

EVAN (*slowly*): Only that the joke's on me. (*Puts note on piano.*)

CHERRY: You're a queer one, aren't you?

EVAN: Possibly. . . . Cherry . . . if Jimmy rags you about a picture I burnt, keep up the mystery. I threw a drawing in the fire and pretended it was you, an absolute masterpiece.

CHERRY: Idiot. Whatever for?

EVAN: Another leg-pull. He thinks I'm a big noise in the artistic world.

CHERRY: So do I.

124

EVAN: Well, don't!

There is a sound of voices from the hall.

CHERRY: There's the doctor. You'd better hurry, or you'll run slap into everybody.

EVAN: Come across the Ferry with me, and put me in the train.

He looks at note on piano again. CHERRY *watches him.*

CHERRY: She may not see it there.

EVAN: Oh, yes, she will. Cherry. Will you do something else for me?

CHERRY: Anything, darling old boy, always. You know that.

EVAN: Play backgammon with Jimmy to-night.

CHERRY: Is *that* all? Of course. You are a funny one.

EVAN (*swiftly*): Come on . . .

They go out through hatch-door. Sound of voices in hall. STELLA *speaking.*

STELLA: I'll see he doesn't move too much, and if you think massage would be good for him I'll get on to that woman in Bodmin. The number's in the book.

JIMMY *comes limping in with stick. Makes his way to sofa, lets himself down carefully. Front door slams.* STELLA *comes into room.*

JIMMY: Thank the Lord that's over. Ham-fisted old blighter.

STELLA: He didn't hurt you too badly, dear. Now lie down and let me prop this cushion behind your back. That's better. Want a drink?

JIMMY: Not at the moment. I'll wait till supper. Six dreary weeks he says I'll be here with this useless foot. What am I going to do all the time?

STELLA: Don't worry, pet. I'll look after you.

JIMMY: It's turned jolly nippy. Throw a log on the fire, will you? Evan's bonfire has put the whole thing out.

STELLA *bends to fire.*

Where *is* Evan? Tell him to come and cheer me up.

STELLA: I expect he's in the studio. I'll call him.

She goes to steps, calls, "Evan," but there is no reply.

JIMMY (*lighting a cigarette, and turning handle of gramophone*): I tell you what we'll do to-night. We'll have a riotous evening, with lots of music. Evan can thump the piano, and I'll play every damn record I can find.

While he speaks and puts on a record, STELLA *finds note on piano, and reads it. She holds note in her hand, and goes to hatch-window, looking out across the harbour. She stands very still, her hands on the ledge of the hatch.*

I'll play some of the old ones that you're fond of. You'd like that, sweetheart, wouldn't you?

He starts playing record from "Annie Get Your Gun." Hums and whistles "I can do Anything better than You can."

What are you doing?

STELLA (*after a moment*): I'm watching the Ferry.

JIMMY: What's it doing?

STELLA: It's half way across the harbour already. In a moment it will reach the other side.

126

JIMMY: Will it? Shut the window, will you? There's a hell of a draught coming down the back of my neck.

STELLA waits a moment, then shuts window and door. She goes to desk, puts the letter in a little drawer and shuts it. Moves down to fireplace, turns on lamp, and then looks at JIMMY.

STELLA: Come on, then, darling, there's time for one game before I go and cope with the supper.

She sits beside JIMMY on the sofa, and rattles the dice. JIMMY hums to record, where raucous woman screams in high-pitched voice:

"Anything you can do I can do better
I can do anything better than you.
No, you can't,
Yes, I can.
No, you can't,
Yes, I can.
No, you can't,
Yes, I can. . . . Yes, I can. . . ."

JIMMY reaches to make first move, saying the words of song, and STELLA sings:

"Yes, I can. . . .
Yes, I can. . . ."

AS THE CURTAIN FALLS

THE END